d for the love of food for the love of food for the love of food for the love of food for the love of food

the love of food for the love of food for the love of food for the love of food for the love of food for the le

d for the love of food for the love of food for the love of food for the love of food for the love of food

the love of food for the love of food for the love of food for the love of food for the love of food for the le

d for the love of food for the love of food for the love of food for the love of food for the love of food

the love of food for the love of food for the love of food for the love of food for the love of food for the le

d for the love of food for the love of food for the love of food for the love of food for the love of food

the love of food for the love of food for the love of food for the love of food for the love of food for the le

od for the love of food for the love of food for the love of food for the love of food for the love of food

the love of food for the love of food for the love of food for the love of food for the love of food for the le

od for the love of food for the love of food for the love of food for the love of food for the love of food

the love of food for the love of food for the love of food for the love of food for the love of food for the le

od for the love of food for the love of food for the love of food for the love of food for the love of food

the love of food for the love of food for the love of food for the love of food for the love of food for the le

od for the love of food for the love of food for the love of food for the love of food for the love of food

the love of food for the love of food for the love of food for the love of food for the love of food for the le

od for the love of food for the love of food for the love of food for the love of food for the love of food

the love of food for the love of food for the love of food for the love of food for the love of food for the le

od for the love of food for the love of food for the love of food for the love of food for the love of food

the love of food for the love of food for the love of food for the love of food for the love of food for the le

od for the love of food for the love of food for the love of food for the love of food for the love of food

r the love of food for the love of food for the love of food for the love of food for the love of food for the le

od for the love of food for the love of food for the love of food for the love of food for the love of food

r the love of food for the love of food for the love of food for the love of food for the love of food for the le

od for the love of food for the love of food for the love of food for the love of food for the love of food

r the love of food for the love of food for the love of food for the love of food for the love of food for the le

od for the love of food for the love of food for the love of food for the love of food for the love of food

r the love of food for the love of food for the love of food for the love of food for the love of food for the le

THE FOODHALL COOKBOOK

– for the love of food –

THE FOODHALL COOKBOOK

– for the love of food –

GRESHAM FERNANDES
KELVIN CHEUNG   POOJA DHINGRA
SABYASACHI GORAI   ZORAWAR KALRA

Photography by Anshika Varma

Foodhall

Lustre Press
Roli Books

ISBN: 978-93-5194-100-2

Published by Roli Books, 2017

M-75, Greater Kailash II Market
New Delhi 110 048, India
Ph: +91-11-4068 2000
Email: info@rolibooks.com
Website: www.rolibooks.com

Design and layout: Misha Oberoi

Printed and bound in India

Contents

Foreword

All throughout history, food has brought people closer and created a sense of identity not only within people but also within nations. Most often on our travels, we explore a country through its cuisine and food culture, thereby giving food tremendous importance. No matter where you go in the world, food will always be the most commonly discussed and bonded over subject that helps create new relationships and renews old ones.

Back in 2011, when we first started Foodhall in Mumbai, we wanted to find a way of providing people with a space that instilled and inspired a sense of community around excellent ingredients and inspirations. I vividly remember my early days at Foodhall, spending time interacting with our shoppers, to really understand what they were looking for. People were not only in search of the best ingredients or exceptional services, but they were looking out for a space where they could feel inspired and rediscover their zeal and feed their passion for food. Over the years, we believe we have upheld the cultural importance of food by catering to customers across different cuisines and nationalities. People from all over the world have come to Foodhall to get in touch with their roots and also discover new tastes and cuisines. Every ingredient picked, every new recipe discovered, every bag checked out, brings joy to a family and fosters new bonds. The belief that Foodhall has the power to inspire people to cook has now compelled us to consider creating our own cookbook.

So after years of being a destination and an experience that provides world-class ingredients spanning various cuisines, we have created a cookbook that is an amalgamation of our thoughts, vision, and never-ending love for food. To celebrate this beautiful relationship with food, we have collected and curated recipes that take you around the world, as you flip through these pages.

Entire sections are curated to let you travel regions through their ingredients, textures and dishes. These experiences are championed by chefs who have made a mark in their respective fields. For instance, Chef Saby's section brims with vivid flavours of the Mediterranean. Gresham's Warm Mushroom Salad showcases the beautiful textures of earthy mushrooms that highlight the simplicity of Modern European cuisine. Kelvin Cheung's delightful Pumpkin Congee is reminiscent of the very popular Indian khichdi with brighter colours and extra crunchiness. Zorawar Kalra's section stays true to Indian cuisine, yet modernizes it to make it cooler and much sexier. To culminate the culinary journey, an entire section devoted to desserts, highlights Pooja Dhingra's expertise, namely Kesar Pista Cupcakes and Falooda-inspired Rose Chia Pudding, our two favourites. Every chef has championed Indian and international ingredients together, to create a distinctly unique food journey that finds its place in *The Foodhall Cookbook*.

Now that we have the best culinary experts and their favourite dishes neatly packed into this book, the final thing that makes it so special is that each and every ingredient mentioned here is available at all Foodhall stores across the country. We wanted to ensure that each of these dishes use wholesome ingredients and have simple preparations to help you recreate restaurant quality meals in the comfort of your own home. As Chef Saby states, 'Foodhall has made cooking easy for professionals as well as for people cooking at home due to the easy availability and variety of ingredients that they have! Be it the most exotic of fruits and vegetables, to cheese, to sauces, to meats to ready mixes, to kitchen equipment and small tools – Foodhall is the one stop destination for everything!'

Foodhall over the years has inspired and enabled many home chefs like me to discover new recipes, cook amazing meals, and indulge loved ones. *The Foodhall Cookbook* is our passionate endeavour to instill the love of food and cooking (and eating!) in each one of you. We hope following these recipes and cooking at home brings you as much joy as it did to us in creating them.

Bon Appétit.

— Avni Biyani
Concept Head, Foodhall

Foodhall

Foodhall

CLASSIC
LAVASH CRISPS

SAFEDA
MANGO

ICE CREAM

MAX
PROTEIN
THE HOUSE O

Pooja Dhingra

MODERN EUROPEAN

by GRESHAM FERNANDES

Besides collecting pulp fiction, comics and knives, I also collect cookbooks – the last two being what inspires me and are core to what I do professionally. The deciding factor lies in who has crafted them, and are they visually appealing?

When Foodhall asked me to contribute for the book, and told me that I could cook in my style, which is modern European, it was a simple choice to make. My cooking style is not very defined in a particular cuisine but is based on common sense and not taking the middle path – Yuzu juice, a Japanese staple replaces lemon in a basic *meunière*, which is a classic French brown butter sauce; other times I would use acidic passion fruit, or the juice of lacto fermented mushrooms to do the job. Use the world as your pantry and taste as you go.

Look at cooking with the five core building blocks – bitter, acidic, sweet, salty and umami. Understand what the ingredients taste in their basic form and then begin building. wEither juxtapose them or combine them to form harmony. Ingredients that have a common core but have different flavours should be switched to create some new exciting flavour combinations. The simple example being honey or maple for sugar, or smoked *bhut jolokia* for chipotle chillies; mind the heat though.

Most of these may or may not work but that's the fun part if you really love cooking. Don't do this if you are crunched for time and have to put food on the table. That's the reason why old recipes have stayed that way. My grandmother had to take care of five kids, the house, and pets in the backyard. She did not have the time to experiment, but made small subtle changes whenever she could.

The dishes here are super simple and based more on taste than measures; if you love things less acidic, reduce the amount but taste as you go – cook with intuition, with seasons being your guide.

Except the roast chicken and the leaf salads a lot of dishes evolve with time, and taste better the next day. Don't get livid with the size of the mushrooms not being perfect or the tomatoes not being the right sweetness – the greatness of a cook lies in turning regular ingredients into another level of greatness.

As for sourcing the ingredients, it is really simple. I find most of them in one place – Foodhall. The placement of the ingredients also helps you build a relationship with them. Keep your eyes open; some ingredients go better with others, but being different is the norm now and you will always have a talking point at your next dinner party.

Hope you enjoy cooking them as I did. *Yoi shokuji o motte imasu*, or have a good meal.

— Gresham Fernandes

Foodhall

PANTRY STAPLES

Essential ingredients you need for these recipes.

- ARUGULA
- BRIE CHEESE
- CHANTERELLE MUSHROOMS
- CHÉVRE
- CHIVES
- COUSCOUS
- ENOKI MUSHROOMS
- FLAXSEEDS
- KALAMATA OLIVES
- KALE
- MIRIN
- OYSTER MUSHROOMS
- PARMA HAM
- PECORINO ROMANO CHEESE
- PORCINI MUSHROOMS
- PORCINI POWDER
- PORTOBELLO MUSHROOMS
- RADICCHIO
- ROSEMARY
- SHIITAKE MUSHROOMS
- SHIMEJI MUSHROOMS
- SORREL
- SWISS CHARD
- THYME
- WATERCRESS

Braised Beetroots with Oranges, Plums and Brie

A hearty salad with spoon tender beetroots, plums and brie cheese flavoured with sweet acidic oranges.

Preparation time: 1½ hours Cooking time: 1 hour Serves: 2

ingredients

4 plums, thinly sliced
6½ tbsp / 100 gm brie cheese, chilled as it helps while cutting

For the braised beetroots:

4 medium-sized beetroots, peeled
Juice and zest of one orange
1 sprig fresh thyme, plucked
Salt and sugar to taste
6½ tbsp / 100 ml olive oil
1 tsp / 5 gm Arqa fennel seeds, toasted
1 tsp / 5 gm Arqa coriander seeds, toasted

For the dressing:

2 tbsp / 30 ml beetroot cooking juices
2 tbsp / 30 ml extra virgin olive oil
1 tbsp / 15 ml balsamic vinegar
Salt and sugar, if required

method

1. **For the braised beetroots**, mix together the beetroots, juice and zest of orange, thyme, salt and sugar to taste, olive oil, fennel seeds and coriander seeds in a bowl. Leave to marinate overnight.
2. Preheat the oven to 200°C / 390°F. Mix the beets again and transfer into a pan with a fitted metal lid (or use aluminum foil instead). Bake in a preheated oven for 45 minutes or until a knife inserted in the beet goes through without resistance. Remove the pan from the oven and allow the beets to cool in the liquid. Cut the beets into slices and let them rest in the same liquid (use the liquid as part of the dressing).
3. **For the dressing**, mix the beetroot cooking juices with the extra virgin olive oil and balsamic vinegar. The additional olive oil adds a hint of fruitiness and freshness to the dish. Season with salt and sugar, if required.
4. Neatly alternate the sliced beets, chilled brie cheese and plums on a serving plate, garnished with any seasonal leaves and the dressing. It also goes well on toast as a crostini.

Spinach, Arugula and Citrus Salad with Granola

A light, green and fruity salad with tender, bitter and peppery leaves accompanied with a healthy, homemade multi-seed and grain granola chunks.

Preparation time: 15 minutes   Cooking time: 30 minutes   Serves: 2

ingredients

For the puffed grain granola:

1 cup / 250 gm puffed grain mix from Traditions by Foodhall
Zest of one orange
4 tbsp / 60 ml honey
1 Arqa Kashmiri dried red chilli, finely chopped
½ tsp / 2½ gm Arqa cinnamon powder
½ tsp / 2½ gm ginger, finely chopped
1 tbsp / 15 gm peanuts, toasted, chopped
1 tbsp / 15 gm Bustaan pistachios, toasted, chopped
½ tsp / 2½ gm flaxseeds, toasted

For the dressing:

4 tbsp / 60 ml olive oil
1 tbsp / 15 gm Dijon mustard paste
2 tbsp / 30 ml orange juice
2 tbsp / 30 ml lemon juice
½ tsp / 2½ gm ginger, chopped
Salt and black pepper to taste

For the salad:

1 bunch baby spinach, washed in cold water, drained
1 bunch arugula, washed in cold water, drained
1 of each, orange and other seasonal citrus fruits, peeled, cut into attractive wedges
2 tbsp / 30 gm Bustaan almonds, toasted, sliced

method

1. **For the puffed grain granola**, preheat the oven to 120°C / 250°F. Mix together the puffed grain mix, orange zest, honey, red chilli, cinnamon powder, ginger, peanuts, pistachios and flaxseeds; pack them tightly in a baking tray. Bake for 30 minutes or till the granola feels dry and brittle. Turn off the heat and let the mix dry. It should feel compact and should break easily.
2. **For the dressing**, mix together the olive oil, mustard paste, orange juice, lemon juice and ginger together. Season with salt and black pepper. Refrigerate.
3. **For the salad**, mix the baby spinach, arugula and the citrus wedges lightly with the dressing. Add the toasted almonds.
4. Serve the salad with broken granola chunks.

Warm Mushroom Salad

An assortment of cooked mushrooms with different textures, served warm garnished with bright and peppery scallions and watercress.

Preparation time: 15 minutes   Cooking time: 5 minutes   Serves: 4

ingredients

6 fresh shiitake mushrooms (if dried, soak in hot water overnight)
150 gm button mushrooms, sliced
1 bunch shimeji mushrooms, whole, bottom ends trimmed
1 bunch oyster mushrooms, sliced
1 bunch enoki mushrooms, whole, bottom ends trimmed
2 fresh portobello mushrooms, sliced
3 tbsp / 45 ml olive oil
1 tsp / 5 gm ginger, finely chopped
1 tsp / 5 gm garlic, finely chopped
1 Arqa Kashmiri dried red chilli, finely chopped
2 scallions, whites only, finely sliced
1 tbsp / 15 ml soy sauce
1 tbsp / 5 ml balsamic vinegar
Salt and black pepper to taste
10 cherry tomatoes, sliced
4 scallions, greens only, sliced
1 bunch fresh watercress leaves or arugula leaves

method

1. Rehydrate the dried mushrooms, if using.
2. Heat a pan till it begins to smoke; add the oil, ginger, garlic, red chilli and scallion whites; sauté quickly.
3. Add the shiitake, button, shimeji, oyster, enoki and portobello mushrooms; toss on high heat. Season with soy sauce, balsamic vinegar, salt and black pepper. Mix in the cherry tomatoes.
4. Serve garnished with the scallion greens and fresh watercress or arugula leaves.

Apple Brie and Parma Ham with Bitter Radicchio

A modern version of an old French classic salad made of apple, cheese, radicchio and parma ham that creates depth of textures and colours with myriad flavours, bitter, sweet, salty, umami and sour - all in one bowl!

Preparation time: 10 minutes | Cooking time: N/A | Serves: 2

ingredients

1 green apple, sliced
½ bunch sorrel, torn
½ head radicchio, torn
½ bunch kale, torn
10 tbsp / 150 gm brie cheese, sliced
3¼ tbsp / 50 gm Bustaan hazelnuts, toasted
4 slices parma ham, thinly sliced

For the dressing:
4 tbsp / 60 ml extra virgin olive oil
1 tbsp / 15 gm Dijon mustard paste
2 tbsp / 30 ml white wine vinegar
Salt, black pepper and sugar to taste

method

1. Compose the salad by adding layers of green apple, sorrel, radicchio, kale, brie cheese, hazelnuts and parma ham to create depth of textures and colours. Keep aside.
2. **For the dressing**, combine together the extra virgin olive oil, mustard paste and white wine vinegar. Season with salt, black pepper and sugar to taste. Whisk well and refrigerate until ready to serve.
3. Serve the salad with the chilled dressing.

Butter Bean Crostini with Salty Pecorino Romano and Parsley

The almost sweet beans contrast the salty pecorino romano superbly. Served on toasted baguette or sourdough with a drizzle of olive oil, this dish makes an excellent appetizer to go with crisp white wine.

Preparation time: 15 minutes + overnight for soaking | Cooking time: 15 minutes | Serves: 4

ingredients

For the beans:

13 tbsp / 200 gm white beans, soaked overnight
Salt and sugar to taste
1 onion, halved
2 sprigs fresh thyme
1 tomato, halved
4 heads garlic, peeled
6 tbsp / 90 ml extra virgin olive oil
1 tbsp / 15 gm butter
Water to cover the beans

For the dressing:

3¼ tbsp / 50 gm pecorino romano cheese
1 tsp / 5 gm fresh chives, chopped
2 tsp / 10 gm fresh flat-leaf parsley
1 tsp / 5 gm garlic, finely minced
4 tbsp / 60 ml extra virgin olive oil
Salt and black pepper, crushed, to taste
Baguette or any sourdough

method

1. Pressure cook the white beans with salt and sugar to taste, onion, thyme, tomato, garlic, extra virgin olive oil, butter and enough water to cover the beans. Cook on high heat till the first whistle then reduce heat to medium and cook for 10 minutes more. Let the cooker depressurize by itself.
2. Strain the liquid but do not discard (this can be used as stock to make a risotto). Discard the onion, thyme and tomato. Lightly mash the beans when warm and mix in the dressing ingredients (pecorino cheese, chives, parsley, garlic and olive oil). Season with salt and black pepper.
3. Serve the beans on toasted baguette or any sourdough and drizzle some more olive oil.

Soy and Mirin Marinated Mushrooms

A robust marinade of assorted mushrooms made with an Asian twist. This tastes better with age and goes well with cheese or grilled pizza or tossed in with just buttered fettuccini.

Preparation time: 15 minutes | Cooking time: 1 minute | Serves: 4

ingredients

2 portobello mushrooms, sliced
1 bunch chanterelle mushrooms, torn
1 bunch oyster mushrooms, whole, if small
10 gm porcini mushrooms, dried
6 shiitake mushrooms, sliced
1 bunch shimeji mushrooms, whole, base trimmed
200 gm button mushrooms, sliced
1 tsp / 5 gm Arqa fennel seeds
1 tsp / 5 gm Arqa coriander seeds
¼ cup / 60 ml Kikkoman soy sauce
1 cup / 250 ml water
1 cup / 250 ml olive oil
¼ cup / 60 ml mirin
10 cloves garlic, peeled
1 sprig fresh rosemary
Salt and black pepper to taste
1 bunch enoki mushrooms, whole, base trimmed

method

1. In a heavy-bottomed pan, add the portobello, chanterelle, oyster, porcini, shiitake and button mushrooms along with fennel seeds, coriander seeds, soy sauce, water, olive oil, mirin, garlic and rosemary.
2. Gradually, bring the mix to the boil on medium heat. Lower heat and cook till 80 per cent of the water is evaporated and the oil floats on top with a dark liquid below. Season with salt and pepper. Remove from heat.
3. Add the enoki mushrooms now as it cooks with the heat of the liquid. Store the mix in a sterilized jar and refrigerate. Leave aside for 2-3 days to enhance the flavour. Reheat and serve as a side dish with grilled meat or on toast as an appetizer.

Prawn with Pickled Shiitake and Soft Scramble

A great appetizer or breakfast dish made of prawns, mushrooms and eggs and yet so different from a regular scrambled egg. This goes well as a topping on toast as well as with steamed rice.

Preparation time: 30 minutes | Cooking time: 40 minutes + 2 days | Serves: 2

ingredients

For the pickled shiitake mushrooms:

6 rehydrated shiitake mushrooms, thinly sliced
2 tbsp / 30 ml soy sauce
2 tbsp / 30 gm sugar
1 cup / 250 ml liquid of soaked shiitake mushrooms
3 tbsp / 45 ml vinegar
½ tsp / 2½ gm ginger, julienned

For the scrambled eggs:

5 organic eggs
Salt, white pepper and sugar to taste
1 tsp / 5 ml soy sauce
½ tsp / 2½ gm fish sauce (optional)
2 tbsp / 30 ml olive oil
8 medium-sized prawns
2 fresh shiitake mushrooms, sliced
2 button mushrooms
½ tsp / 2½ gm fresh red chilli, finely chopped
¼ tsp ginger, finely chopped
1 tsp / 5 gm garlic, finely chopped
1 scallion, white and green, sliced into rounds
1 loaf French bread

method

1. **For the pickled shiitake mushrooms**, add the shiitake mushrooms, soy sauce, sugar, liquid of soaked mushrooms, vinegar and ginger to the pan and cook on low heat for half an hour. Remove and keep aside for 2 days to let the pickling solution mature and soften. (This makes extra, it can also be used as topping for fish, crostinis, salad, stews, etc.)
2. Beat the eggs with the salt, pepper, sugar, soy sauce and fish sauce (optional).
3. Heat the oil in a pan; sauté the prawns, shiitake and button mushrooms with the red chilli, ginger and garlic. Season to taste. Cook till done.
4. Remove the pan from the heat and keep aside to cool. The best scrambled eggs start in a cold pan.
5. Add the egg mixture in the same cold pan with the mushrooms and prawns, and cook on very low heat, mixing continuously to break the egg curd. Cook till a light porridge-like consistency is achieved. Add the scallion and pickled shiitake mushrooms.
6. Toast the bread with a drizzle of olive oil.
7. Serve the toasted bread topped with the egg mix.

Caramelized Onion and Chèvre Flatbread with Kalamata Olives and Arugula

Slow-cooked, almost melt-in-the-mouth onions served on top of long fermented bread with chèvre, olives and arugula. Robust flavours – goes well with red wine.

Preparation time: 3 hours + overnight refrigeration | Cooking time: 30 minutes | Serves: 4

ingredients

For the bread (makes extra):
2 cups / 500 gm refined flour
½ tsp / 2½ gm fresh yeast
½ tsp / 2½ gm sugar
Salt to taste
Water as required

For the caramelized onions:
1 kg onions, sliced
⅓ cup / 85 ml olive oil
2 tbsp / 30 gm butter
A few sprigs fresh thyme, picked
1 tbsp / 15 gm garlic, sliced
Salt and black pepper to taste
½ tsp / 2½ gm sugar
Generous amount of chèvre (goat cheese)
2 tbsp / 30 gm Kalamata olives, julienned
6-8 leaves arugula
A few Arqa pink peppercorns

method

1. **For the bread**, combine together the flour, yeast, sugar, salt and water in a bowl; knead into a dough. Refrigerate overnight to proof. Remove the dough the next day and knock it back. Keep aside to rise in a warm place.

2. **For the caramelized onions**, heat the butter and olive oil in a pan; add the onions and cook, covered, on low heat for 5 minutes. Add the thyme and garlic; keep stirring, in intervals, to prevent the onions from burning. Cook till soft and tender. Season with salt, black pepper and sugar.

3. Preheat the oven to 250°C / 490°F. Roll out the dough to ½ inch thickness. Bake in the oven till it rises, forms bubbles and is aerated, do not fully cook it. Remove from the oven and while still hot, brush the bread with olive oil. Add the caramelized onion and top with *chèvre* (goat cheese). Bake again till the edges are toasty. Add the olives, arugula, pink peppercorns and some more chèvre, if required.

4. Serve hot.

Sweet Potato and Ragi Gnocchi with Braised Leaves

Ragi, the new super grain, makes great gnocchi with sweet potatoes. A healthy dish of gnocchi coated with lemon sauce and mixed with braised leaves. This dish can also be made with sweet potato leaves.

Preparation time: 2 hours | Cooking time: 10 minutes | Serves: 4

ingredients

For the gnocchi:

2 large sweet potatoes
1 cup / 250 gm ragi flour
¼ cup / 60 gm parmesan cheese
1 egg
Salt and black pepper to taste

For the lemon sauce:

¼ cup / 60 ml water
⅓ cup / 85 gm butter, chilled
¼ cup / 60 gm parmesan cheese
1 tbsp / 15 gm zest of lemon
1 tbsp / 15 gm fresh parsley
Lemon juice to taste

For the braised leaves:

4 tbsp / 60 ml extra virgin olive oil
4 cloves garlic, sliced
1 onion, sliced
1 small green chilli, diced
4 kale leaves
1 bunch romaine lettuce
2 leaves Swiss chard
1 radish, top only (optional)
2 beetroots, top only (optional)
4 mustard leaves
Salt, black pepper and sugar to taste
½ tsp / 2½ gm fresh basil, chopped
½ tsp / 2½ gm fresh oregano, chopped

method

1. **For the gnocchi**, preheat the oven to 200°C / 390°F. Roast the sweet potatoes with skin in the oven on high heat till a skewer inserted goes through without force. Peel the sweet potatoes while still warm and pass through a potato press. In a bowl, mix the sweet potatoes with the ragi flour, parmesan cheese, egg, salt and black pepper to taste. Divide the mix equally into small balls and roll each out on the back of a fork with little pressure to form the classic gnocchi shape. Repeat till all are done. Boil the gnocchi in water till they begin to float. Remove and cool in iced water; strain. Keep aside.
2. **For the lemon sauce**, gently heat the water till it comes to the boil. Slowly incorporate the chilled butter till a thick coating sauce-like consistency is formed. Add the parmesan cheese, lemon zest, parsley and lemon juice; season and keep aside.
3. **For the braised leaves**, heat the olive oil in a pan; add the garlic, onion and green chilli, sauté. Add the kale leaves, lettuce, Swiss chard, radish leaves, beetroot top and mustard leaves; cook till the leaves begin to wilt. Add the salt, pepper and sugar to taste; cook on medium heat till the excess water evaporates. Lastly add the basil and oregano.
4. In the same pan, add the gnocchi and cook on low heat till warm. Add the lemon sauce, some more parmesan cheese, pepper and the herbs. Do not boil the sauce as it will split. Serve hot.

Chef's Tip: *If you are a vegetarian, use egg replacer instead of eggs.*

Beet and Barley Risotto with Roasted Walnut Butter and Dill

A lactose-free dish made with barley, a texture very different from risotto rice. A hearty risotto dish tossed in walnut butter and topped with toasted walnuts and berries. Goes well with poached fish too.

Preparation time: 1 hour   Cooking time: 20 minutes   Serves: 4

ingredients

For the walnut butter (makes extra):

1 cup / 250 gm Bustaan walnuts, toasted till slightly brown
6½ tbsp / 100 ml vegetable oil
Salt and black pepper to taste

For the vegetable stock (makes extra):

1 medium-sized carrot, halved
1 medium-sized onion, halved
4 cups / 1 lt water
2 tomatoes, halved
1 stalk celery
Salt and sugar to taste

For the risotto:

1 cup / 250 gm barley, washed, soaked overnight
4 tbsp / 60 ml olive oil
1 medium-sized onion, chopped
½ tbsp / 8 gm garlic, chopped
½ tbsp / 8 gm leeks, chopped
½ tbsp / 8 gm celery, chopped
2 medium-sized beets, diced
1 cup / 250 ml red wine
½ tbsp / 8 gm dill, chopped
Berries (mulberries, strawberries or dried cranberries) for garnishing

method

1. **For the walnut butter**, rub the toasted walnuts between 2 kitchen cloths to remove most of the skin. Keep some aside for garnishing. Purée the walnuts with the oil till a smooth sauce-like consistency is achieved; season with salt and black pepper.
2. **For the vegetable stock**, char the carrot and onion, cut side down, on a dry pan, till golden brown. Add the water, tomatoes, celery, salt and sugar; bring to the boil. Reduce heat and simmer for 45 minutes or till the broth tastes good. Strain, and add more seasoning, if required.
3. **For the risotto**, heat the olive oil in a pan; add the onion, garlic, leeks and celery; sauté till fragrant. Add the beets and deglaze with the wine. Reduce till almost syrup-like consistency. Add the soaked barley and toss to coat. Add the warmed stock in parts till the barley is plump. Toss in some toasted walnuts, walnut butter and season to taste. Add the dill and mix well.
4. Serve topped with seasonal berries (mulberries, strawberries or dried cranberries).

Buckwheat Crêpe with Roasted Vegetable and Parmesan Fondue

Thin French crêpes made with buckwheat flour, stuffed with roasted vegetables and topped with parmesan fondue, a great gluten-free dish.

Preparation time: 1½ hours | Cooking time: 30 minutes | Serves: 2

ingredients

For the crêpes:

1 cup / 250 gm buckwheat flour
¼ cup / 60 ml milk or as required for the batter
2 eggs
A pinch Arqa nutmeg
Salt to taste
1 tsp / 5 gm ghee

For the roasted vegetables:

1 onion, not peeled
2 tomatoes, halved
1 yellow bell pepper
1 zucchini, diced into big pieces
3 tbsp / 45 ml extra virgin olive oil
4 cloves garlic, peeled, chopped
½ tsp / 2½ gm fresh parsley, chopped
½ tsp / 2½ gm oregano

For the parmesan fondue:

¼ cup / 60 gm parmesan cheese, grated
½ cup / 125 ml milk
½ cup / 125 ml cream
Salt and black pepper to taste

method

1. **For the crêpes**, mix together the buckwheat flour, milk, eggs, nutmeg, salt and ghee to a smooth batter, add more milk if required. To make crêpes, heat a non-stick 12 inch-skillet over medium heat; lightly coat with butter. Add ⅓ cup batter and swirl to completely cover the bottom of the skillet. Cook for 2-3 minutes or until the underside is golden brown. This makes about 6-8 crêpes. Store between clean, damp kitchen cloths to prevent drying.
2. **For the roasted vegetables**, heat the oven to 250°C / 480°F. Roast the whole onion (without covered in foil) till soft. Remove, peel and cut into quarters; keep aside. Do the same with the tomatoes till the skin bursts and are slightly brown. Peel, chop and store with the onion. Roast the pepper till soft and brown. Peel, chop and store the juices. Oil and season the zucchini; roast the same way.
3. Heat the olive oil in a pan; add the garlic and cook till light golden. Add the roasted vegetables and cook, covered, for 15 minutes on low heat. Add the parsley, oregano and seasoning.
4. **For the parmesan fondue**, heat the milk and cream in a pan till it just comes to the boil. Remove and keep aside to cool. When cool enough to handle, add the grated parmesan, return the pan to heat and warm the sauce again, whisking well. Season with salt and black pepper.
5. Stuff each crêpe with the roasted vegetables and top with the parmesan fondue or serve on the side.

Saffron Chickpea Stew with Grilled Vegetables and Chilli Soffrito

An untraditional chickpea and couscous dish served with fire-grilled vegetables. A Spanish take on a Moroccan staple.

Preparation time: 2 hours | Cooking time: 30 minutes | Serves: 4

ingredients

For the chickpea stew:

1 cup / 250 gm chickpeas from Traditions by Foodhall, soaked
6-8 strands Arqa saffron
5 tbsp / 75 ml olive oil
½ cup / 125 gm onions, chopped
2 tbsp / 30 gm garlic, chopped
½ cup / 125 gm tomatoes, grated
1 tsp / 5 gm Arqa paprika

For the garlic oil (makes extra):

1 tbsp / 15 gm garlic, chopped
½ tsp / 2½ gm fresh rosemary, chopped
½ tsp / 2½ gm fresh parsley, chopped
½ cup / 125 ml olive oil
Zest of one lemon

For the grilled vegetables:

2 wedges pumpkin, sliced
4 green asparagus, sliced
1 each coloured pepper, whole
1 zucchini, sliced
1 carrot, sliced
1 cherry tomato
2 potatoes, halved

For the couscous:

1 cup / 250 gm couscous
Water as required
2 tbsp/ 30 ml olive oil
¼ tsp Arqa turmeric powder
½ tsp / 2½ gm Arqa Madras curry powder
1 tbsp / 15 gm fresh mint, chopped
1 tbsp / 15 gm fresh green coriander, chopped
Salt to taste

method

1. **For the chickpea stew**, pressure cook the chickpeas with salt and enough water to cover for 10 minutes on high pressure. Remove and keep aside to cool in the cooker. Save the water and chickpeas separately.
2. Toast the saffron in a pan till it is just warmed through. Keep aside.
3. Heat the olive oil in a heavy-bottomed pan; add the onions and garlic and cook on low heat, till light brown. Add the tomatoes and cook till the water evaporates and the oil floats on top. Add the paprika and toasted saffron, cook for another minute. Add the chickpeas and mix well. Pour in the chickpea stock and cook till a thick gravy is achieved. Adjust the seasoning. Keep aside.
4. **For the garlic oil**, add the garlic, rosemary, parsley and olive oil in a pan; cook on low heat till the garlic turns light brown. Mix in the lemon zest. Keep aside to cool; strain and use as required.
5. **For the grilled vegetables**, marinate the pumpkin, asparagus, coloured peppers, zucchini, carrot, cherry tomato and potatoes with the garlic oil and cook on a heated grill till tender. Mix with the garlic oil again to freshen it up.
6. **For the couscous**, (follow the packet instructions to cook the couscous). Heat the olive oil in a pan; add the turmeric powder and Madras curry powder; cook for a couple of seconds till a fragrant aroma emanates. Add this to the steamed couscous along with the mint and green coriander; mix well.
7. Serve the spiced couscous with the grilled vegetables and chickpea stew.

Charred Broccoli and Pak Choi Tossed with Fermented Black Beans, Lemon and Toasted Almonds

A healthy umami-laden dish with charred and smokey vegetables tossed with fermented black beans and toasted almonds. It is great to eat by itself or as a side too!

Preparation time: 2 hours | Cooking time: 5 minutes | Serves: 4

ingredients

2 heads broccoli, cut into large florets
6 small pak choi, halved
Olive oil for marinating
Salt to taste
Red chillies, deseeded, for garnishing
2 tbsp / 30 gm Bustaan almonds, toasted, sliced

For the dressing:

1 tbsp / 15 gm fermented black beans, soaked in warm water for 2 hours, water discarded
⅛ tsp garlic
1 red chilli
⅛ tsp ginger
1 tsp / 5 ml soy sauce
½ tsp / 2½ ml sesame oil
Juice of one lemon

method

1. Marinate the broccoli florets and pak choi with olive oil and salt.
2. Heat a grill pan with minimum oil; grill the vegetables till charred and tender. Remove and keep aside.
3. **For the dressing**, crush the garlic, red chilli and ginger in a mortar and pestle. Add the black beans and crush again lightly. Add the soy sauce, sesame oil and lemon juice; mix well.
4. Toss the charred vegetables with the black bean dressing, red chillies and almonds; serve hot.

Braised Chicken with Porcini, Balsamic Onions and Roast Potatoes

Slow-cooked, rustic farmer-styled chicken with woody porcini mushrooms and roast potatoes, a one-pot dish that goes well with crusty sourdough bread.

Preparation time: 2 hours | Cooking time: 30 minutes | Serves: 2

ingredients

2 whole chicken legs, with bone and skin, 2 cuts each at the joint, drumsticks and thighs
Salt and black pepper to taste
1 tsp / 5 gm porcini powder
2 tbsp / 30 gm refined flour
4 tsp / 20 gm butter
2 tsp / 10 gm porcini mushrooms, soaked
¼ cup / 60 ml port wine
¼ cup / 60 ml red wine
1 cup / 250 ml chicken stock
⅓ cup / 85 ml cream
1 tsp / 5 gm fresh parsley, chopped

For the balsamic onion:
2 onions, thickly sliced
2 tbsp / 30 ml olive oil
4 heads garlic, crushed
½ tbsp / 8 gm fresh rosemary, chopped
Salt to taste
½ tbsp / 8 gm sugar
4 tbsp / 60 ml red wine
1 tbsp / 15 ml balsamic vinegar

For the roast potatoes:
4 potatoes, peeled, cut into large pieces
2 sprigs fresh rosemary
2 tbsp / 30 ml olive oil
1 tbsp / 15 gm butter
Salt to taste

method

1. **For the balsamic onion**, heat the olive oil in a pan; add the garlic and rosemary and cook till the oil is flavoured. Remove the garlic. Add the onions, salt and sugar; cook till the onions begin to brown. Add the red wine and balsamic vinegar; cook on high heat till the sauce is reduced and coat the onions. Season and keep aside.

2. **For the roast potatoes**, boil the potatoes in salted water till tender. Drain, toss in the colander till bruised. Coat with the whole rosemary, olive oil and butter. Bake in the oven at 160°C / 320°F till golden brown. Reserve the oil that is left after cooking the potatoes (use it when cooking the chicken or for future use when making eggs or grilling vegetables).

3. **For the chicken**, season the chicken with salt and black pepper. Add the porcini powder and flour, mix till well coated. Heat the butter till foaming and cook the chicken till brown. Remove and keep in a colander kept over a bowl to collect the juices.

4. In the same pan, add the soaked porcini mushroom, stir to coat. Add the wines and cook till reduced to syrup-like consistency. Add the chicken stock and juices collected from the chicken; cook till reduced to half. Add the balsamic onion and chicken; cook on low heat for 10 more minutes. Season to taste; stir in the cream and chopped parsley.

5. Serve hot with roast potatoes.

Roast Chicken with Water Chestnut and Pickled Slaw

A great dish to show off one's roasting skills. Tender roast chicken served with sweet and sour pickled slaw and roasted vegetables.

Preparation time: 6 hours | Cooking time: 1½ hours | Serves: 2

ingredients

For the chicken:

1 whole chicken with skin, cleaned, washed, dried with paper, refrigerated uncovered for 6 hours
Salt and black pepper to taste
Zest of one large lemon
Extra virgin olive oil as required
4-5 sprigs fresh rosemary
4-5 sprigs fresh thyme

For the pickled slaw:

1 small cabbage, finely julienned
1 green apple, finely julienned
5 canned water chestnuts, thinly sliced
Salt to taste
¼ cup / 60 gm sugar
¼ cup / 60 ml white wine vinegar
¼ cup / 60 ml white wine
¼ cup / 60 ml water
4 dill stems
2 tbsp / 30 ml vegetable oil
½ tsp / 2½ gm Arqa mustard seeds

For the roasted vegetables:

1 head broccoli, cut
6 brussel sprouts
4 mushrooms, cut
2 potatoes, cut
1 onion, sliced
1 carrot, cut
Salt and black pepper to taste
Olive oil as required
½ tsp / 2½ gm fresh parsley, chopped

method

1. **For the pickled slaw**, mix together the cabbage, green apple and water chestnuts with some salt. Keep aside. Bring the salt, sugar, white wine vinegar, white wine, water and dill stems to the boil in a pan. In another pan, temper the oil with the mustard seeds. Pour this hot oil over the vinegar mix and stir to combine. Pour this warm liquid over the sliced vegetables, mix to coat well. Let it marinate overnight for the flavours to develop. Make sure the vegetables are pressed down and covered by the pickling liquid.
2. **For the roasted vegetables**, season the broccoli, brussel sprouts, mushrooms, potatoes, onion and carrot with salt, pepper, olive oil and parsley.
3. **For the chicken**, season the chicken, inside and outside, with salt and pepper. Mix the olive oil with the lemon zest and massage the chicken well again with this oil. Stuff the chicken with some of the vegetables kept aside for roasting. Add the rosemary and thyme and truss the chicken with a twine. Roast the chicken in a pan for half an hour till a slight colour appears on the breast. Remove the chicken and rest for 10 minutes on a rack.
4. In the same pan, toss the remaining vegetables ensuring that they are coated with the juice of the chicken. Lay the chicken back on the vegetables, drizzle some more olive oil and roast again for another half an hour.
5. Let the chicken rest for half an hour before it is cut.
6. Serve with the pickled slaw and roasted vegetables.

Seafood Risotto with Brown Rice

A spiced seafood and unpolished brown rice risotto, enriched with slow-roasted garlic purée, chilli and fennel.

Preparation time: 1½ hours   Cooking time: 30 minutes   Serves: 2

ingredients

¾ cup / 185 gm brown rice from Traditions by Foodhall, soaked for 1 hour
150 gm king fish, fillets, cut into large chunks, seasoned
4 scallops
2 whole squids, cleaned
4 prawns
2 tbsp / 30 ml olive oil
½ bulb fresh fennel
½ tsp / 2½ gm fennel, dried
1 fresh red chilli
4 heads garlic, sliced
1 onion, sliced
¼ cup / 60 ml white wine
2 cups / 500 ml fish stock
2 tbsp / 30 gm cold butter
¼ cup / 60 gm parmesan cheese
Zest of one lemon

For the roasted garlic cream:
4 heads garlic
4 tbsp / 60 ml olive oil
¼ cup / 60 ml cream
1 sprig fresh thyme
Salt to taste
Juice of one lemon

method

1. Heat the olive oil in a pan; fry the seasoned fish, scallops, squids and prawns, in batches, till it takes some colour but is not fully cooked. Keep aside.
2. In the same pan, add the fennel, chilli, garlic and onion; cook till the onion is translucent. Add the white wine and cook till reduced to syrup-like consistency. Add the rice and the boiled fish stock; cook till the rice absorbs all the liquid. Remove the pan from the heat.
3. **For the roasted garlic cream**, slow roast the garlic pods in a medium-hot oven till the insides turn to mush/ purée. Slice the stem end of the garlic and press the soft roasted garlic out. Purée with the olive oil, cream, thyme leaves and salt till a smooth emulsion is obtained; adjust the taste with lemon juice.
4. Mix this garlic cream with the rice. Add the cold butter, parmesan cheese, lemon zest and the cooked fish, scallops, squids and prawns; serve.

ASIAN

by KELVIN CHEUNG

I love cooking Asian food at home because it appeals to a mass audience, it's familiar to the Indian palate, and it's quite easy once you figure out the prep ahead of time. Since 90 per cent of the work of cooking an Asian meal at home is the preparation, and once you have this down it's a breeze. My biggest tip for any of the following recipes is to have your vegetables pre-cut and ready to go the night or morning before cooking a big meal, especially when entertaining guests. It saves you time and stress! You can also buy pre-packaged, pre-cut vegetables at Foodhall to save time while you are picking up the exotic essentials necessary for cooking my recipes in this book, like soy sauce, oyster sauce, sesame oil, and rice noodles. Foodhall has an amazing selection for each item and I am sure you are able to find exactly what you are looking for.

My absolute favourite recipe to make is the sesame spinach chicken salad because it is light, refreshing, and super quick and simple to make. It's the perfect quick lunch or after workout meal for me and I could easily eat this every day. For my home dinner parties, I always make mapo tofu since it appeals to both vegetarians and non-vegetarians and requires nearly zero prep. Once you get the hang of seasoning it to your liking, it's the quickest and most satisfying meal ever. Throw on a pot of rice on the stove or in the rice cooker, and you can get this ready in minutes.

Want to know a secret about cooking Asian cuisine? Because of its unique flavours, you can easily adapt and change the recipes on a whim. Making Asian food is essentially based on theory so the flavour profiles are achieved always by balance. The key to remember is sweet, salty, sour, bitter, and spice! This is very similar to Indian cuisine which also uses the theory of balance in dishes.

Many of the recipes here have drawn inspiration from my upbringing, including favourites my mother liked to cook while we were growing up, working in my father's kitchen throughout my childhood, and current favourites that I make at home with my wife. I hope these recipes find their way to your table and also help build a setting for wonderful memories, just like mine.

Happy cooking!

— Kelvin Cheung

Foodhall

PANTRY STAPLES

Essential ingredients you need
for these recipes.

- ASPARAGUS
- CANDIED WALNUTS
- CAYENNE PEPPER
- CHINESE BLACK VINEGAR
- CHINESE WINE
- HOISIN SAUCE
- JALAPENOS
- KIMCHI
- KOREAN GOCHUJANG
- MAPLE SYRUP
- MISO
- OYSTER SAUCE
- PAK CHOI
- PONZU SAUCE
- RICE WINE VINEGAR
- SAMBAL OELEK
- SILKEN TOFU
- SMOKED PAPRIKA
- SRIRACHA
- SUSHI RICE
- SZECHUAN PEPPERCORNS
- TAHINI
- VANILLA BEAN
- WASABI POWDER

Wasabi Cucumber Salad with Shredded Chinese Cabbage and Pak Choi

A spicy green salad with an acidic kick. This dish can be made into a complete meal by adding eggs or tofu.

Preparation time: 15 minutes | Cooking time: N/A | Serves: 1-2

ingredients

For the salad:

½ head Chinese cabbage, julienned
4-5 pieces baby pak choi, julienned
1 large Asian pear (Granny Smith or any other crunchy fruit), julienned
1 cup / 250 gm musk melon, julienned
½ seedless cucumber, peeled, diced
2 scallions, thinly sliced
1 cup / 250 gm mung bean sprouts, washed

For the dressing:

1 cup / 250 ml mayonnaise
6½ tbsp / 100 ml rice wine vinegar
3¼ tbsp / 50 gm wasabi powder
3 tbsp / 45 ml sesame oil
2 tsp / 10 ml lemon juice
Kosher salt and black peppercorns, freshly ground, to taste

method

1. **For the dressing**, combine together the mayonnaise, rice wine vinegar, wasabi powder, sesame oil and lemon juice in a blender. Whisk until fully incorporated; season with salt and pepper. Keep aside.
2. **For the salad**, soak the cabbage and pak choi in a gallon of water. When the vegetables start floating, change the water at least once to ensure it is thoroughly cleaned. Remove and transfer the vegetables into a salad spinner. Refrigerate until ready to serve.
3. Just before serving, put the pear and musk melon into a large mixing bowl. Add the cabbage, pak choi, cucumber, scallions and mung bean sprouts; toss gently with 2-3 tbsp of the dressing. Season with salt and pepper; serve immediately.

Sesame Spinach Chicken Salad

A light, healthy refreshing chicken and spinach salad packed with texture and crunch.

Preparation time: 15 minutes | Cooking time: 15 minutes | Serves: 1-2

ingredients

1 pc chicken breast, julienned, cooked or poached
Salt and black pepper to taste
1 red onion, julienned
150 gm baby spinach, washed
2 tbsp / 30 gm candied walnuts
2 tsp / 10 gm sesame seeds

For the dressing:
¼ cup / 60 ml rice wine vinegar
¼ cup / 60 gm sesame seeds, toasted
2 tsp / 10 ml soy sauce
1 tbsp / 15 gm tahini
2 tsp / 10 ml honey
1 knob ginger, grated
½ cup / 125 ml vegetable oil
¼ cup / 60 ml sesame oil
Salt and black pepper to taste

method

1. Season the chicken with salt and black pepper. Pan sear or just simply poach it in water or stock for about 10-12 minutes or till cooked. Remove and allow to cool completely.
2. **For the dressing**, blend together the rice wine vinegar, sesame seeds, soy sauce, tahini, honey and ginger in a blender till smooth. Slowly drizzle both the vegetable oil and sesame oil till emulsified. Season with salt and black pepper. Keep aside.
3. Combine the cooked chicken and red onion in a mixing bowl and season lightly with salt and pepper. Drizzle the dressing and mix gently. Add the baby spinach and arrange the chicken pieces on top.
4. Serve garnished with candied walnuts, sesame seeds and a bit more of the dressing.

Ginger Soba Noodle Salad Ponzu Dressing

A chilled noodle salad flavoured with confit ginger-scallion oil is not only refreshing but also an ultimate comfort food.

Preparation time: 25 minutes | Cooking time: 20 minutes + 1 hour for steeping | Serves: 2-4

ingredients

1 pack dry noodles (Ramen or instant noodles)
1 knob ginger, peeled, minced
1 bunch scallions, washed, chopped
⅓ cup / 85 ml olive oil
1 tbsp / 15 ml sesame oil
1 cup / 250 gm daikon or white radish, grated
2 tbsp / 30 gm sesame seeds, toasted
2 cucumbers, peeled, deseeded, diced into small pieces
2 tbsp / 30 ml light soy sauce
¼ cup / 60 gm ponzu

For the garnishing:
3 tbsp / 45 gm peanuts, toasted, chopped
3 tbsp / 45 gm scallion greens only, chopped

method

1. **For the confit ginger scallion oil**, in a small pot, add the ginger, scallions and olive oil and bring to simmer; remove from heat. Allow to steep for at least an hour.
2. In a pot of boiling water, cook the noodles according to package instructions. When done, remove from heat and drain the water; shock the noodles in ice water. Strain as much as possible; toss the noodles with sesame oil and cool immediately.
3. Place the cooled noodles in a bowl; add the daikon or white radish, sesame seeds, cucumbers, confit ginger scallion oil and season with soy sauce and ponzu. Toss well.
4. Serve garnished with peanuts and scallion greens.

Kimchi Tacos

Flour tortillas stuffed with cabbage kimchi, topped with cheddar cheese, sour cream and a dash of hot sauce.

Preparation time: 20 minutes Cooking time: 15 minutes Serves: 1-2

ingredients

1 cup / 250 gm homemade cabbage kimchi
1 cup / 250 gm cottage cheese (*paneer*), crumbled
2 tbsp / 30 ml vegetable oil / ghee
2 tsp / 10 gm garlic, minced
2 tsp / 10 gm ginger, minced
2 tbsp / 30 gm Korean gochujang
Salt and black pepper to taste
Flour tortillas or homemade chapattis

For the garnishing:

2 tbsp / 30 gm cheddar cheese, grated (or any other cheese of your choice)
2 tsp / 10 gm scallions, chopped
Sour cream
Sriracha sauce

method

1. Heat the oil or ghee in a sauté pan on low to medium heat; cook the garlic and ginger for 2-3 minutes. Add the kimchi and cottage cheese; sauté for a few more minutes.
2. Add the Korean gochujang and toss till evenly coated. Add salt and pepper to taste; mix well. Remove and keep the filling aside.
3. In a separate pan, add a touch of oil or ghee to toast and heat the tortillas. Transfer the tortilla on to a plate and assemble the taco with the above filling.
4. Serve garnished with cheddar cheese, scallions, sour cream and hot sauce.

Moo Shu Chicken

An iconic American-Chinese appetizer, Moo shu chicken is tortilla served with Chinese-style chicken filling – a perfect blend of taco-style eating with classic Chinese flavours.

Preparation time: 25 minutes · Cooking time: 15 minutes · Serves: 2-3

ingredients

200 gm chicken / prawns / mushrooms, shredded (use any one)
2 tbsp / 30 ml vegetable oil
150 gm green cabbage, shredded
100 gm red cabbage, shredded
3¼ tbsp / 50 gm carrots, shredded
3¼ tbsp / 50 gm scallion greens only, cut into 3-inch batons
2 tbsp / 30 gm garlic, sliced
2 tsp / 10 gm green chillies, minced
3 tbsp / 45 ml hoisin sauce
1 tbsp / 15 ml oyster sauce
2 tsp / 10 ml dark soy sauce
Salt and black pepper to taste
5-6 flour tortillas or lettuce cups to serve in

method

1. Sauté chicken or prawns / mushrooms till fully cooked. Remove and transfer into a bowl.
2. Heat the oil in a pan; sauté the green and red cabbage until just starting to wilt. Then add the carrots, scallion greens, garlic and green chillies; sauté for another 3-4 minutes.
3. Once the vegetables are al dente, add the hoisin sauce, oyster sauce and dark soy sauce; toss well.
4. Add the chicken and season with salt and pepper. Toss well.
5. Serve with tortillas or in lettuce cups.

Mapo Tofu Szechuan Peppercorns

A classic Szechuan dish of tofu, mushrooms and green beans with a spicy twist.

Preparation time: 15 minutes | Cooking time: 10 minutes | Serves: 1-2

ingredients

1¼ cups / 300 gm silken tofu, diced into big pieces
5 tsp / 25 ml sesame oil
2 tsp / 10 gm ginger, sliced
2 tsp / 10 gm cloves garlic, sliced
50 gm or 25 gm jalapenos, sliced, or green chillies (adjust the spice level as desired)
6½ tbsp / 100 gm mushrooms, sliced
¼ cup / 60 gm green beans, cut
6½ tbsp / 100 ml vegetable stock
2 tbsp / 30 ml sambal oelek
5 tbsp / 75 ml oyster sauce
2 tsp / 20 ml dark soy sauce
1 tbsp / 15 gm Arqa Szechuan peppercorns, freshly ground
4 tbsp / 60 gm corn starch
2 scallions, thinly sliced

method

1. Heat the sesame oil in a pan on low to medium heat; add the ginger, garlic and jalapenos or green chillies (as desired); sauté until fully cooked.
2. Add the mushrooms and sauté for 4-5 minutes. Add the green beans and sauté for another minute. Add the vegetable stock along with sambal oelek, oyster sauce, dark soy sauce and Szechuan pepper; mix well. Bring to the boil.
3. Add the diced tofu and heat through.
4. Make a slurry with the corn starch and quickly stir in to prevent the mix from forming lumps.
5. Serve hot, garnished with sliced scallions and a dash of sesame oil.

Szechuan Eggplants

Blanched eggplants flavoured with garlic, tossed in Chinese black vinegar and accompanied with steamed rice.

Preparation time: 20 minutes   Cooking time: 10 minutes   Serves: 2-3

ingredients

4 Chinese eggplants, diced
2 tbsp / 30 ml vegetable oil
5 tsp / 25 gm cloves garlic, sliced
4 tsp / 20 gm ginger, sliced
5 Arqa dried red chillies
¼ cup / 60 ml Chinese black vinegar
3 tbsp / 45 ml oyster sauce
2 scallions, minced

method

1. Run the diced eggplants under cold water to prevent oxidizing; strain and allow to dry.
2. In a deep stock pot, blanch the eggplant, in small batches. Remove and drain on absorbent kitchen paper towels.
3. Heat the oil in a large wok; sauté the garlic, ginger and dried red chillies for about 2-3 minutes. Add the blanched eggplants and while tossing on medium to high heat, add the Chinese black vinegar and oyster sauce, toss until fully absorbed.
4. Serve garnished with scallions and accompanied with rice.

Szechuan-style Asparagus and Lotus Root with Homemade Szechuan Peppercorn Chilli Oil

A flavourful asparagus and lotus root dish whipped in a jiffy – usually served with steamed jasmine rice.

Preparation time: 15 minutes   Cooking time: 10 minutes   Serves: 1

ingredients

1 bunch asparagus, cut into 2-inch batons
2-3 lotus roots, peeled, blanched in salted water for 1 minute to remove bitterness
1 bunch Chinese broccoli, sliced on a bias cut 2 inch
3 tbsp / 45 ml vegetable oil
2 Arqa dried red chillies, minced
10 cloves garlic, minced
½ tsp / 2½ gm sugar
1 tsp / 5 ml soy sauce
A dash Chinese wine
1 tsp / 5 gm Arqa Szechuan peppercorns, freshly ground
2 tsp / 10 ml oyster sauce

method

1. Heat the oil in a pan on medium heat; add the minced chillies and cook on low heat, until the oil turns red (about 2-3 minutes).
2. Add the garlic and fry until cooked but still transparent. Season with sugar and soy sauce.
3. Add the Chinese broccoli and sauté for 2 minutes. Now add the asparagus and blanched lotus roots and deglaze with Chinese wine. Taste and reseason with Szechuan pepper and oyster sauce and serve hot.

Kung Pao Shrimps

A spicy hot dish from northern China warms the stomach and mouth. Kung pao shrimp is laced with peanut-laden sauce to give that extra crunch.

Preparation time: 20 minutes | Cooking time: 15 minutes | Serves: 1-2

ingredients

16-20 pcs / 350 gm shrimps, peeled, deveined
3 tbsp / 45 ml vegetable oil
5 Arqa dried red chillies
1 bunch scallion greens only
1 cup / 250 gm scallion bulbs, sliced
6½ tbsp / 100 gm red onions, sliced
3¼ tbsp / 50 gm garlic, sliced
1½ tbsp / 25 gm fresh red chillies, minced
2 tbsp / 30 ml hoisin sauce
2 tbsp / 30 ml oyster sauce
1 tbsp / 15 ml Sriracha (or any other hot sauce)
1 cup / 250 gm peanuts, roasted

method

1. Heat the oil till smoking hot in a hot pan; add the shrimps and sear for 30 seconds. Remove and reserve.
2. In the same pan, add the dried red chillies, scallion greens and bulbs, red onions, garlic, and chillies; sweat for 3-4 minutes.
3. Add the shrimps back in along with hoisin sauce, oyster sauce, Sriracha and peanuts; toss well.
4. Continue to sauté and toss till evenly coated. Cook till all the sauces are absorbed.
5. Serve hot with steamed rice.

Vegetable Pad See Ew

The much loved Thai street food, pad see ew is made with rice sticks, vegetables and tofu and flavoured with soy sauce and peanuts.

Preparation time: 2 hours | Cooking time: 15 minutes | Serves: 2-3

ingredients

¼ pack rice sticks, soaked for at least 2 hours in cold water to hydrate
2 tbsp / 30 ml vegetable oil
1 egg (optional)
3¼ tbsp / 50 gm garlic, sliced
3¼ tbsp / 50 gm onions, sliced
1½ tbsp / 25 gm red chillies, fresh or dried, minced
1 pack tofu, firm, fried till crisp (add chicken or prawn for variation)
1 cup / 250 gm cabbage, julienned
1 cup / 250 gm carrots, julienned
2 tbsp / 30 ml vegetarian oyster sauce
1 tbsp / 15 ml dark soy sauce
1 tsp / 5 gm sugar
½ cup / 125 gm peanuts, roasted, chopped
1 cup / 250 gm basil, roughly chopped
⅓ cup / 85 gm scallions, chopped

method

1. Bring a pot full of water to the boil.
2. Heat the pan to medium-high heat and add the oil. If using egg, scramble and add it now along with garlic, onions, chillies and tofu; sweat for 3 minutes.
3. Add the cabbage and carrots; sauté for 3 minutes until wilted.
4. Meanwhile, add the noodles to the pot and boil for 1 minute. Remove the pot and strain until all the water has drained. Add the noodles to the pan and toss until well mixed.
5. Add the oyster sauce, dark soy sauce and sugar; toss until the sugar is dissolved and the sauce is incorporated.
6. Toss in the chopped peanuts, basil and scallions; serve immediately.

Dandan Noodles

This fiery Szechuan noodle in vegetable broth is classically served with minced meat. But the earthy umami packed mushrooms is a good substitute.

Preparation time: 2 hours | Cooking time: 45 minutes | Serves: 2-4

ingredients

1 pack dry rice sticks, soaked for 2 hours in cold water
8 cups / 2 lt vegetable stock
3 Arqa dried red chillies, chopped
6 fresh red or green chillies, chopped
2 stalks lemon grass, chopped
10 cloves garlic, sliced
3 cups / 750 gm peanuts, roasted
2 cups / 500 ml coconut milk

For the mushroom duxelles:
1 kg mushrooms, de-stemmed, chopped
2 tbsp / 30 ml vegetable oil
10 cloves garlic, minced
4 fresh red or green chillies, chopped
3 tbsp / 45 gm Arqa Szechuan peppercorns
2 tbsp / 30 ml dark soy sauce

For the garnishing:
2 tbsp / 30 gm scallions, chopped
Hot sauce or chilli oil, as desired

method

1. In a large stock pot, add the vegetable stock; dried red chillies, fresh chillies, lemon grass and garlic cloves; simmer for 30-40 minutes. Then add 2½ cups peanuts and coconut milk; simmer till the peanuts turn soft. Remove the pot from the heat and blend the broth in a blender; strain and season with salt and pepper.
2. **For the mushroom duxelles**, in a large, hot pan heat the oil and sauté the mushrooms until all the liquid is absorbed. Add the minced garlic, fresh chillies and Szechuan peppercorns; sauté for 4-5 minutes. Season with dark soy sauce.
3. In a separate pasta pot, boil the noodles according to package instructions until just cooked. Remove and place in a soup bowl. Pour the hot broth over the noodles.
4. Serve garnished with mushroom duxelles, remaining chopped peanuts, scallions and a dash of hot sauce or chilli oil.

Pumpkin Congee

A perfect Sunday brunch, this dish is a Chinese equivalent to the Indian khichdi *and is made of pumpkin purée and rice.*

Preparation time: 30 minutes   Cooking time: 1 hour   Serves: 2-4

ingredients

1 kg fresh pumpkin, seeded, peeled, diced into medium-sized pieces
8 cups / 2 lt water or vegetable stock
1 knob ginger, peeled, sliced
3/4 cup / 185 gm jasmine sweet rice from Traditions by Foodhall, rinsed well
Salt, white pepper and light soy sauce for seasoning
1 cup / 250 gm pumpkin seeds, roasted
½ cup / 125 ml chilli oil (for garnishing only)
½ cup / 125 gm scallions, chopped
¼ cup / 60 gm fresh green coriander, chopped

method

1. Bring the water or vegetable stock to the boil in a pot. Add the pumpkin and ginger; simmer until the pumpkin is tender. Remove half the pumpkin and mash or purée and reserve.
2. In the same pot, add the rice and simmer until fully cooked (it takes about an hour or so). Now stir in the pumpkin purée.
3. Season with salt, white pepper and light soya sauce; mix well.
4. Serve garnished with roasted pumpkin seeds, chilli oil, scallions and green coriander.

Mango Sticky Rice with Miso Caramel

A sticky rice dessert topped with mangoes, miso caramel sauce and some coconut sauce served along with sesame muesli to bring in the savoury element.

Preparation time: 45 minutes | Cooking time: 1 hour | Serves: 4-5

ingredients

2-3 fresh mangoes, peeled, chopped

For the coconut sauce:
2 cups / 500 ml coconut milk
1¾ tbsp / 25 gm sugar
½ tbsp / 8 gm salt
1 cup / 250 ml ginger juice

For the sticky rice:
1½ cups / 375 gm Thai sticky rice / Sushi rice from Traditions by Foodhall
½ cup / 125 gm sugar
1 tbsp / 15 gm salt
1 stalk lemon grass
1 knob ginger
1 vanilla bean
1 cup / 250 ml coconut milk

For the miso caramel sauce:
½ cup / 125 gm sugar
2 tbsp / 30 ml water
2 tbsp / 30 gm miso

For the sesame muesli:
400 gm Bustaan cashew nuts
400 gm Bustaan almonds
400 gm sesame seeds
400 gm peanuts
300 gm coconut, desiccated
2 tbsp / 30 ml sesame oil
½ tbsp / 8 ml pure maple syrup
½ tsp / 2½ gm sea salt, fine grained
¼ tsp Arqa smoked paprika
¼ tsp Arqa cayenne pepper

method

1. **For the coconut sauce**, add the coconut milk, sugar, salt and ginger juice in a pan. Reduce heat and simmer gently until thick and infused. Keep aside.
2. **For the sticky rice**, rinse the rice well and take 8/10 of the weight of the rice in water and bring to the boil. Add the rice, sugar, salt, lemon grass, ginger and vanilla bean; reduce heat to low, cover and steam until all the water is evaporated (it takes about 20 minutes) and the rice is cooked. Pour in the coconut sauce (reserve some for topping) and continuously fold and fan without mashing until absorbed and cooled.
3. **For the miso caramel sauce**, add the sugar and water into the pot. Cook the sugar till almost hard to crack, to a dark caramel (177°C / 350°F this is the temperature of the caramel). Remove from heat and whisk in the miso. Reserve until ready to serve.
4. **For the sesame muesli**, mix together the cashew nuts, almonds, sesame seeds, peanuts, coconut, sesame oil, maple syrup, sea salt, smoked paprika and cayenne pepper; roast in the oven at 160°C / 320°F for 20 minutes or until golden brown, stir twice during roasting.
5. **To assemble**, serve the rice at room temperature and make large piles on the plate. Place some chopped mangoes on each pile of rice and drizzle miso caramel sauce and some coconut sauce (kept aside).
6. Serve garnished with the sesame muesli.

CONTEMPORARY INDIAN

by ZORAWAR KALRA

Indian cuisine reflects over 5000 years of history, encompassing an array of native regional sub-cuisines that have developed over centuries, influenced by various cultural interactions through trade relations and more importantly, a resultant effect of numerous foreign invasions. It was these influences that the natives were introduced to new ingredients, preparation methods and cooking techniques, including the use of unique spices and tea, especially the use of saffron as a hallmark seasoning in many dishes. This resulted in the culinary influence and diversity of regional cuisine and flavours found across modern-day India.

As an avid lover of the robustness that Indian food offers, I take immense pride in our cuisine and believe that it needs to be reintroduced to the world. Among the most notable contributions to Indian food in recent years, has been the introduction of modernist culinary techniques.

Aside from the radical changes in the menus and food across many new Indian restaurants, globally, the cuisine has also gained ground owing to the popularity of media, its reach and various successful programmes on food and cooking. Most of them have shown a different, more creative aspect of Indian food, with a fine balance between traditional and modern preparations and their presentation – laying emphasis on utilizing 'all the five senses' while dining.

The advent of concepts like Foodhall has given easy access to produce and ingredients of international quality to home cooks and chefs, thereby assisting them in trying out exotic, restaurant-style and quality dishes. Offering an exhaustive and fresh range of ingredients, exotic fruits, cheeses, unique Indian and international spices, and uncommon vegetables, all under one roof, Foodhall is definitely a go-to store for enthusiastic home chefs, inviting them to explore contemporary Indian food.

It is time for us to take our culinary heritage forward by imbibing cutting edge, new cooking techniques, working with ingredients from all over the world that renew the everyday home dining experience. With that thought, I hope that these recipes help the readers and ardent home chefs to dabble with creativity, experiment with global flavours, and recreate the magic of modern Indian food.

And remember, *food is not just a hobby, it is pure passion.*

— Zorawar Kalra

Foodhall

PANTRY STAPLES

Essential ingredients you need for these recipes.

- AVOCADO
- BIRD-EYE CHILLIES
- CHORIZO
- COCONUT MILK
- GALANGAL
- GOAT CHEESE
- HUNG YOGURT
- KAFFIR LIME
- MINT CHUTNEY
- MOZZARELLA CHEESE
- NIHARI MASALA
- PAPDI
- PARMESAN CHEESE
- PIRI-PIRI SAUCE
- PHYLLO SHEETS
- PINE NUTS
- PINK PEPPERCORNS
- QUINOA
- SAFFRON
- SEV
- TAMARIND CHUTNEY
- ZUCCHINI

Avocado Papdi Chaat

A fusion of traditional Indian street food made with crisp, fried flour discs (papdi) topped with spiced chickpeas, yogurt, mint and tamarind chutney along with feta cheese and Mexico's most popular fruit 'avocado'.

Preparation time: 20 minutes   Cooking time: 20 minutes   Serves: 2

ingredients

For the chaat:

2 cups / 500 gm chickpeas from Traditions by Foodhall, boiled
½ tsp / 2½ gm Arqa chaat masala
1 tsp / 5 gm black salt
1 tsp / 5 gm salt
½ tbsp / 8 gm Arqa cumin powder
1 tsp / 5 gm black pepper
1½ tsp / 7 gm sugar
½ tsp / 2½ gm Arqa garam masala

To serve:

50 gm *papdi*
5 tsp / 25 gm yogurt
3¼ tbsp / 50 gm mint chutney
2 tsp / 10 gm tamarind chutney
1 tbsp / 15 gm avocado, diced
4 tsp / 20 gm pomegranate seeds
4 tsp / 20 gm feta cheese, crumbled
1 tsp / 5 gm *sev*
Micro greens, any variety, for garnishing

method

1. **For the chaat**, mix the boiled chickpeas with the chaat masala, black salt, salt, cumin powder, black pepper, sugar and garam masala in a large bowl.

2. To serve, crush the *papdi* on a plate. Add the yogurt, mint and tamarind chutney over it. Serve garnished with diced avocado, pomegranate seeds, feta cheese, fried *sev* and the micro greens.

Red Curry Paneer Tikka

Soft chunks of fresh cottage cheese cooked in a clay-oven, mixed with the traditional Thai red curry and complemented with the refreshing flavour of basil.

Preparation time: 30 minutes   Cooking time: 30 minutes   Serves: 4

ingredients

1 cup / 250 gm cottage cheese (*paneer*)

For the first marinade:

Salt to taste
1 tbsp / 15 gm ginger-garlic paste

For the second marinade:

4 tsp / 20 gm hung yogurt
2 tsp / 10 ml mustard oil
2 tsp / 10 gm Arqa red chilli powder
½ tsp / 2½ gm Arqa cardamom powder

For the red curry:

4 tsp / 20 gm bird-eye chillies
½ tbsp / 8 gm galangal
2 tsp / 10 gm leek
½ tbsp / 8 gm celery
1 tsp / 5 gm ginger
½ tsp / 2½ gm kaffir lime leaves
4 tsp / 20 ml olive oil
2 tsp / 10 gm garlic, chopped
2 tsp / 10 gm seasoning powder
2 tsp / 10 ml honey
1 tsp / 5 gm peanut butter
½ tsp / 2½ gm lemon grass
2 tsp / 10 ml dark soy sauce
1 tsp / 5 ml coconut milk
2 tsp / 10 gm corn flour (optional)

For the basil chutney:

10 tbsp / 150 gm fresh basil
½ tsp / 2½ ml olive oil
A few cloves garlic
½ tsp / 2½ gm parmesan cheese
A few pine nuts
1 tsp / 5 gm hung yogurt
½ tsp / 2½ gm salt
½ tsp / 2½ gm black pepper

method

1. **For the first marinade**, marinate the cottage cheese with salt and ginger-garlic paste.
2. **For the second marinade**, combine the hung yogurt with mustard oil, red chilli powder and cardamom powder. Add the cottage cheese and turn the pieces to coat well. Leave to marinate for about 30 minutes. Skewer the cottage cheese in a tandoor and cook until golden.
3. **For the red curry**, boil the red chillies along with galangal, leek, celery, ginger and kaffir leaves. Remove and allow to cool. Then grind to a fine paste. Heat the oil in a Chinese wok; sauté the garlic. Add the fine red curry paste and cook until dry. Add the seasoning powder, honey, peanut butter, lemon grass and dark soy sauce; mix well. Pour in the coconut milk and cook till the consistency thickens. Add the corn flour dissolved in 2 tsp water to thicken, if needed. Remove and keep aside.
4. **For the basil chutney**, blanch the basil in hot water and strain. Make an emulsion of olive oil, garlic, parmesan cheese and pine nuts in a blender. Add the blanched basil into the blender along with the hung yogurt to make chutney. Add salt and black pepper and adjust the consistency.
5. Mix the red curry with the *paneer tikka* in a bowl.
6. Serve garnished with micro greens and accompanied with basil chutney.

Makai and Malai Phyllo Rolls

Thin unleavened dough - phyllo pastry - derived from Balkan cuisine stuffed with sweetcorn kernels and tossed in rich creamy Punjabi malai *gravy.*

Preparation time: 25 minutes   Cooking time: 5 minutes   Serves: 4

ingredients

6½ tbsp / 100 gm corn
2 tbsp / 30 gm Amul cheese, grated
4 tsp / 20 ml cream
2 tbsp / 30 gm bell pepper, chopped
½ tsp / 2½ gm salt
½ tsp / 2½ gm black pepper
1 tsp / 5 gm oregano
9 (10 cm x 10 cm) phyllo sheets
4 tsp / 20 gm butter
Vegetable oil for frying
Edible flowers and home-grown cress for garnishing

method

1. Blanch the corn in hot water and strain. Allow to cool.
2. When cool, roughly chop the corn and mix in the cheese, cream and bell pepper.
3. Season with salt, pepper and oregano, adjust the flavours of the mixture.
4. Line the phyllo sheets with melted butter and arrange them one on top of the other in a stack.
5. Stuff the corn mixture and roll it into small rolls, giving it an even shape.
6. Heat the oil in a pan; deep-fry the stuffed phyllo rolls at 180-200°C until golden brown. Remove and drain the excess oil on absorbent kitchen paper towels.
7. Serve hot garnished with edible flowers and home-grown cress and accompanied with any dip.

Chicken Tikka and Caesar Salad Lettuce Rolls

Tender chicken marinated in tandoori masala, cooked on open fire over charcoal, rolled in crisp lettuce, drizzled with traditional Mexican 'Caesar' dressing and topped with parmesan shavings.

Preparation time: 30 minutes | Cooking time: 20 minutes | Serves: 4

ingredients

250 gm chicken thighs, cut each into 4 pieces

For the marinade:

1 tsp / 5 gm Arqa mace powder
1 tsp / 5 gm Arqa cardamom powder
½ tbsp / 8 gm Arqa garam masala
2 tsp / 10 gm Arqa red chilli powder
½ cup/ 60 gm hung yogurt
5 tsp / 25 gm salt
2 tsp / 10 gm ginger paste
2 tsp / 10 gm garlic paste
6½ tbsp / 100 gm butter for basting

To serve:

4 lettuce (iceberg or romaine), cleaned, roughly torn into 3-inch pieces, refrigerate
8 tsp / 40 mm mayonnaise
4 tsp / 20 gm piri-piri sauce
Parsley, chopped, for garnishing
6 tbsp / 90 gm parmesan cheese, grated

method

1. **For the marinade**, marinate the chicken thighs with mace powder, cardamom powder, garam masala, red chilli powder, hung yogurt, salt, ginger and garlic paste for about 2 hours.
2. Spread the chicken pieces on a baking tray and bake at 250°C / 480°F for about 15-18 minutes, basting twice in between with butter.
3. Remove the chicken pieces and allow to cool.
4. Spread the lettuce on a flat surface. Drizzle mayonnaise and piri-piri sauce over each. Put one piece of the chicken tikka on each lettuce, roll and arrange on a platter.
5. Serve garnished with chopped parsley and grated parmesan.

Goat Cheese Stuffed Zucchini with Mint Powder

Soft cheese chevre, tempered with tangy Indian spices, rolled in zucchini strips and fried.

Preparation time: 30 min   Cooking time: 30 min   Serves: 2

ingredients

300 gm zucchini, cleaned, cut lengthwise into thin strips
400 gm goat cheese, grated
3¼ tbsp / 50 gm Amul processed cheese, grated
4 tsp / 20 gm fresh green coriander, chopped
10 tbsp / 150 gm fresh mint, chopped
2 tsp / 10 gm roasted peanut powder
½ tsp / 2½ gm Arqa red chilli powder
1 tsp / 5 gm Arqa cumin powder
3¼ tbsp / 50 gm Arqa chaat masala
1 tsp / 5 gm black pepper
½ tsp / 2½ gm Arqa coriander powder
½ tbsp / 8 gm ginger, chopped
½ tsp / 2½ gm garlic, chopped
6½ tbsp / 100 gm salt
6½ tbsp / 100 gm fresh mint leaves (for powder)
Vegetable oil for frying

method

1. Mix the goat cheese and Amul cheese well together.
2. Add the green coriander, mint and roasted peanut powder to the mix.
3. Add the red chilli powder, cumin powder, chaat masala, black pepper, coriander powder, ginger and garlic; mix well. Adjust the salt.
4. Divide the cream cheese mix into 10 portions of 30 gm each.
5. Place a portion on a thin zucchini strip and roll into a thin cylinder. Repeat till all are done.
6. **For the mint powder**, place the fresh mint into a dehydrator at 35°C for 6-8 hours. Crush into fine powder and store in an airtight container. Use as required.
7. Heat the oil in a pan; place the zucchini cylinders, one by one, and cook evenly. Remove and drain the excess oil on absorbent kitchen paper towels. Repeat till all are fried.
8. Serve hot sprinkled with home-made mint powder.

Baingan Bharta Ratatouille

The classic north Indian delicacy made from smoked eggplant, mashed and flavoured with Indian spices.

Preparation time: 15 minutes | Cooking time: 15 minutes | Serves: 2

ingredients

500 gm large eggplants
3¼ tbsp / 50 ml mustard oil
1 tbsp / 15 gm ginger, chopped
½ tsp / 2½ gm cloves garlic, chopped
3¼ tbsp / 50 gm onions, chopped
1 cup / 250 gm tomatoes, chopped
1 tsp / 5 gm salt
1 tsp / 5 gm Arqa cumin powder
1½ tsp / 7 gm Arqa turmeric powder
2 tsp / 10 gm Arqa red chilli powder
1 tsp / 5 gm Arqa chaat masala
1 tsp / 5 gm Arqa garam masala
4 tsp / 20 gm ghee
1 tbsp / 15 gm fresh green coriander, chopped

method

1. Char the whole eggplants in a tandoor until completely cooked and easy to peel; mash and keep aside.
2. Heat the mustard oil in a medium-sized pan; add the ginger and garlic. Cook until brown.
3. Add the onions, tomatoes and salt; cook until the onions turn translucent.
4. Add the cumin powder, turmeric powder, red chilli powder and chaat masala; cook until the spices release their aroma.
5. Mix in the mashed eggplant along with the garam masala, ghee and green coriander.
6. Serve hot.

The Original Dal Makhani

The popular Punjabi dish made from slow-cooked black lentils and red kidney beans, simmered in the richness of cream, butter and mild Indian spices.

Preparation time: 15 minutes | Cooking time: 2 hours | Serves: 2

ingredients

6½ tbsp / 100 gm split black gram (*urad dal*) from Traditions by Foodhall, cleaned, washed, soaked overnight
1 tbsp / 15 gm kidney beans from Traditions by Foodhall, cleaned, washed, soaked overnight
2 tsp / 10 gm Bengal gram (*chana dal*) from Traditions by Foodhall, cleaned, washed
13 tbsp / 200 gm ghee
½ tbsp / 8 gm ginger paste
1 tsp / 5 gm garlic paste
1 tbsp / 15 gm Arqa red chilli powder
½ tbsp / 8 gm Arqa cumin powder
1 tsp / 5 gm Arqa coriander powder
6½ tbsp / 100 gm tomato purée
Salt to taste
3¼ tbsp / 50 ml fresh cream
4 tsp / 20 gm butter
½ tsp / 2½ gm Arqa dry fenugreek leaves

method

1. Pressure cook the split black gram, kidney beans and Bengal gram with salt and enough water to cover for about 45 minutes, approximately 4 whistles, or till thoroughly cooked.
2. Heat the ghee in a heavy-bottomed pan; add the ginger paste, garlic paste, red chilli powder, cumin powder and coriander powder. Cook till the spices release their aroma.
3. Add the tomato purée and cook further till the oil separates from the spices. Stir in the boiled dal and adjust the salt.
4. Remove and transfer the dal into a bowl. Serve hot topped with cream, butter and dry fenugreek leaves.

Lamb Shank Nihari

A flavourful meaty stew, native to Old Delhi, made with slow-cooked lamb shanks, along with bone marrow, to extract the rich flavours of the meat into the mildly spiced stew.

Preparation time: 30 minutes   Cooking time: 1½ hours   Serves: 2

ingredients

4 pcs lamb shanks
3¼ tbsp / 50 gm ghee
2 cups / 500 gm onions, sliced
3¼ tbsp / 50 gm salt
2 tbsp / 30 gm ginger-garlic paste
1 tsp / 5 gm Arqa turmeric powder
3 Arqa bay leaves
3¼ tbsp / 50 gm gram flour
¼ cup / 60 gm yogurt
Fresh green coriander
for garnishing

For the spice mix:
3 Arqa black cardamoms
4 Arqa green cardamoms
1 Arqa cinnamon stick
20 gm Arqa mace
1 Arqa clove
10 tbsp / 150 gm Arqa cumin powder
4 tsp / 20 gm Arqa coriander powder
2 tsp / 10 gm Arqa garam masala
or
4 tsp / 20 gm *nihari* masala

method

1. **For the spice mix**, grind the black and green cardamoms, cinnamon stick, mace and clove in a grinder and then mix in the cumin powder, coriander powder and garam masala. Keep aside and use as required.
2. Heat the ghee in a heavy-bottomed pan; add the meat and cook till brown. Remove from the pan.
3. In the same pan, add the onions and salt. Sweat the onions till translucent and the colour starts turning brown. Add the ginger-garlic paste, turmeric powder and bay leaves; sauté till cooked. Remove the pan from the heat.
4. Blend the gram flour with the yogurt (yogurt is blended so as to prevent it from curdling) before adding it to the pan.
5. Stir in the spice mix or *nihari* masala. Add the lamb and braise till the meat gets cooked and becomes tender. Cook, covered to prevent the aroma from escaping. Reduce heat and simmer the meat.
6. Serve hot, garnished with chopped green coriander.

Teen Mirchi ka Paneer

Fresh cottage cheese scrambled with Indian spices and herbs, stuffed in bell pepper and capsicum, cooked in a tandoor and served on a bed of creamy Indian gravy.

Preparation time: 20 minutes | Cooking time: 30 minutes | Serves: 4

ingredients

2 nos / 60-75 gm red bell pepper, halved lengthwise, seeds discarded
2 nos / 60-75 gm yellow bell pepper, halved lengthwise, seeds discarded
2 nos / 60-75 gm capsicum, halved lengthwise, seeds discarded
2 tbsp / 30 ml olive oil

For the stuffing:

350 gm cottage cheese, grated
2 tbsp / 30 gm ghee
1 tsp / 5 gm Arqa cumin seeds
2 tbsp / 30 gm onions, chopped
1 tbsp / 15 gm ginger, chopped
2 tsp / 10 gm garlic, chopped
1 tsp / 5 gm green chillies, chopped
2 tbsp / 30 gm tomatoes, deseeded, chopped
2 tsp / 10 gm Arqa turmeric powder
2 tsp / 10 gm Arqa red chilli powder
1 tsp / 5 gm Arqa coriander powder
1 tbsp / 15 gm fresh green coriander, chopped
1 tsp / 5 gm Arqa garam masala
2 tsp / 10 ml lemon juice

For the crust:

3¼ tbsp / 50 gm Amul cheese, grated
3¼ tbsp / 50 gm bread crumbs
Black peppercorns, freshly ground, to taste
1 tbsp / 15 gm fresh green coriander, chopped

method

1. **For the stuffing**, heat the ghee in a pan; crackle the cumin seeds. Add the onions and cook till translucent. Add the ginger, garlic and green chillies; sauté for 2 minutes on medium heat until the raw flavour of garlic disappears. Add the tomatoes, turmeric powder, red chilli powder and coriander powder. Cook on low heat until the masala leaves ghee from the sides. Add the grated cottage cheese and cook for 30 seconds or until the mixture is hot. Turn down the heat and mix in the green coriander, garam masala and lemon juice.
2. **For the crust**, mix the Amul cheese, bread crumbs, black pepper and green coriander in a bowl with light hands keeping it dry and crumbly.
3. Drizzle some olive oil over the bell peppers and let it marinate for 5 minutes.
4. Pack each half of the red and yellow bell peppers and capsicum with the cottage cheese filling.
5. Place the stuffed bell peppers on a baking tray, open side up. Cover the top with the crust mix and bake at 180°C / 350°F for 12-15 minutes.
6. Remove and serve hot with any chutney as desired.

Malabar Prawn Curry

Kerala-style prawn stew tempered with south Indian favourites - curry leaves, mustard seeds and ginger, and scented with coconut milk extraction.

Preparation time: 20 minutes Cooking time: 20 minutes Serves: 4

ingredients

250 gm prawns, cleaned, shelled
6½ tbsp / 100 gm fresh coconut, grated
5 tsp / 25 gm Arqa whole red chillies
1 tsp / 5 gm Arqa coriander seeds
2 tbsp / 30 gm ghee
1 tsp / 5 gm Arqa mustard seeds
15 curry leaves
1½ tsp / 7 gm garlic, chopped
1 tsp / 5 gm Arqa turmeric powder
1 tsp / 5 gm Arqa cumin powder
½ cup/ 60 ml coconut milk
2 tsp / 10 gm ginger, chopped
Fresh green coriander, chopped for garnishing
½ tsp / 2½ gm black pepper, crushed

method

1. Dry roast the fresh coconut (keep some aside for garnishing) with whole red chillies and coriander seeds. Remove and blend to a fine paste in a grinder.
2. Heat the ghee in a medium-sized pan; add the mustard seeds, curry leaves and garlic. Cook till brown. Add the turmeric powder and cumin powder; sauté till the spices are cooked.
3. Add the red chilli-coconut paste; mix well.
4. Add the prawns and stir-fry. This will infuse the flavour of the curry into the prawns. Add the coconut milk and ginger; reduce heat to low and simmer for 5 minutes.
5. Serve the curry hot garnished with fresh coriander leaves, crushed black pepper and freshly grated coconut.

Mozzarella and Oregano Tawa Parantha

Shallow-fried whole wheat Indian bread stuffed with oregano-flavoured cheese influenced by the Italian and Asian flavours.

Preparation time: 20 minutes | Cooking time: 30 minutes | Serves: 4-6

ingredients

2 cups / 500 gm whole wheat flour
2 tbsp / 30 gm mozzarella cheese, grated
1 tsp / 5 gm oregano
½ tsp / 2½ gm Arqa cumin powder
2 tsp / 10 gm Arqa coriander powder
1 tsp / 5 gm salt
½ tsp / 2½ gm black pepper
5 tsp / 25 ml soya oil
1 tsp / 5 gm ginger, chopped
2 tsp / 10 gm garlic, chopped

method

1. In a big bowl, mix the whole wheat flour with some water and knead into a soft dough. Add more water, if required. Cover and keep aside.
2. Mix the mozzarella cheese with oregano, cumin powder, coriander powder, salt and pepper.
3. Heat the oil in a heavy-bottomed pan; sauté the ginger and garlic till golden brown. Remove and mix this with the cheese mix.
4. Divide the dough into equal portions of 50 gm each.
5. Shape each portion into a round ball. Make a depression in the middle and stuff the cheese mix, sealing the filling inside. Roll the ball into a round disc. Shallow-fry the *parantha* on a griddle until brown on both sides. Remove and repeat till all are done.
6. Serve hot with saffron and mint raita (see recipe on pg. 114).

Honey Chilli Potato Tandoori Parantha Coated with Toasted Sesame Seeds

Whole wheat Indian bread stuffed with honey-chilli potato, cooked in a tandoor and sprinkled with toasted sesame seeds.

Preparation time: 30 minutes   Cooking time: 20 minutes   Serves: 4-6

ingredients

2 cups / 500 gm whole wheat flour
5 tsp / 25 ml soya oil
1 tsp / 5 gm ginger, chopped
2 tsp / 10 gm garlic, chopped
2 tbsp / 30 gm fresh red chillies, chopped
½ tsp / 2½ gm Arqa cumin powder
2 tsp / 10 gm Arqa coriander powder
2 cups / 500 gm potatoes, boiled, grated
1 tsp / 5 gm tomato ketchup
½ tsp / 2½ ml Tabasco sauce
3¼ tbsp / 50 ml honey
1 tsp / 5 gm salt
½ tsp / 2½ gm black pepper
4 tsp / 20 gm Arqa sesame seeds, toasted

method

1. In a big bowl, mix the whole wheat flour with some water and knead into a soft dough. Add more water, if required. Cover and keep aside.
2. Heat the oil in a heavy-bottomed pan; sauté the ginger, garlic and red chillies till the ingredients release their aroma. Add the cumin powder and coriander powder; mix thoroughly.
3. Add the boiled potatoes, tomato ketchup and Tabasco sauce to give tanginess to the filling. Mix with honey and season with salt and pepper. Remove and keep aside.
4. Divide the dough into equal portions of 50 gm each.
5. Shape each portion into a round ball. Make a depression in the middle and stuff the potato mix, sealing the filling inside. Roll the ball into a round disc. Cook the parantha in the tandoor until brown on both sides. Repeat till all are done.
6. Serve hot sprinkled with toasted sesame seeds.

Quinoa Pulao, Pan Tossed Asparagus and Cherry Tomatoes

Protein rich and gluten-free grain, quinoa, tempered with Indian flavours, topped with pan-tossed Dutch asparagus and cherry tomatoes.

Preparation time: 20 minutes Cooking time: 20 minutes Serves: 2

ingredients

6½ tbsp / 100 gm quinoa from Traditions by Foodhall, boiled, drained
5 tsp / 25 ml soya oil
1 tsp / 5 gm Arqa mustard seeds
½ tsp / 2½ gm curry leaves
2 tsp / 10 gm split black gram (*urad dal*) from Traditions by Foodhall
1 tsp / 5 gm red bell pepper, chopped
2 tsp / 10 gm fresh green coriander, chopped
1 tsp / 5 gm salt
½ tsp / 2½ gm Arqa black pepper
2 tsp / 10 ml lemon juice
½ tsp / 2½ gm cherry tomatoes
Banana crisps for garnishing

method

1. Heat the soya oil in a medium-sized pan; add the mustard seeds, curry leaves and split black gram. Stir-fry for a few seconds (keep a few fried curry leaves aside for garnishing).
2. In the same pan, add the bell pepper and green coriander to make it aromatic.
3. Add the boiled quinoa and toss to mix with the condiments and spices.
4. Season with salt, black pepper and lemon juice.
5. Serve garnished with cherry tomatoes, fried curry leaves and banana crisps.

Chorizo Pulao

A popular rice dish from Goa made with steamed long-grained rice, tossed in home-made Goan spices and Spanish pork sausages, chorizo.

Preparation time: 15 minutes   Cooking time: 30 minutes   Serves: 2

ingredients

100 gm chorizo, cubed
2 cups / 500 gm Basmati rice from Traditions by Foodhall
5 tsp / 25 ml soya oil
1 tsp / 5 gm ginger, chopped
2 tsp / 10 gm garlic, chopped
½ tsp / 2½ gm Arqa cumin powder
2 tsp / 10 gm Arqa coriander powder
1 tsp / 5 gm salt
Black pepper, crushed, to taste
1 tsp / 5 gm fresh green coriander, chopped

method

1. Boil the Basmati rice in a heavy-bottomed pan. Remove and keep aside.
2. Heat the soya oil in a separate pan; add the ginger and garlic and cook till golden brown. Add the cumin powder and coriander powder; cook till each spice releases its aroma.
3. Add the cubed chorizo and sear it with the cooked spices.
4. Add the boiled rice; mix well. Season with salt and crushed black pepper.
5. Serve garnished with green coriander.

Red Chillies and Guava Raita, Pink Peppercorn and Pomegranate Raita, Saffron and Mint Raita

Yogurt based dips, spiced with aromatic condiments, accompanying Indian food, served in three contrasting flavours with a mix of fresh fruits, herbs and spices.

Preparation time: 20 minutes Cooking time: N/A Serves: 4

ingredients

2 cups / 500 gm hung yogurt
1 tsp / 5 gm ginger, finely chopped
2 tsp / 10 gm garlic, finely chopped
1 tsp / 5 gm salt
½ tsp / 2½ gm sugar
2 tsp / 10 gm Arqa cumin powder
1 tsp / 5 gm black pepper
½ tsp / 2½ gm fresh green coriander, finely chopped

For the red chilli-guava raita:
5 tsp / 25 gm guava, diced
2 tbsp / 30 gm fresh red chillies, finely chopped

For the pink peppercorns and pomegranate raita:
1 tsp / 5 gm Arqa pink peppercorns
3¼ tbsp / 50 gm Arqa pomegranate seeds

For the saffron and mint raita:
15-20 Arqa saffron strands
1 tbsp / 15 gm fresh mint leaves, chopped

method

1. Cream the yogurt, using a whisk. Mix in the ginger, garlic, salt, sugar, cumin powder, black pepper and green coriander.
2. **For the red chilli-guava raita**, combine the guava and red chillies with the yogurt mix. Serve chilled.
3. **For the pink peppercorns and pomegranate raita**, combine the pink peppercorns and pomegranate seeds with the yogurt mix. Serve chilled.
4. **For the saffron and mint raita**, combine the saffron and chopped mint leaves with the yogurt mix. Serve chilled.

MEDITERRANEAN

by SABYASACHI GORAI

My recipes in this book are based on Mediterranean cuisine. I have travelled all over Spain, France, Italy and Africa numerous times and have tried to incorporate these recipes with the Mediterranean essence in this book. Home cooking inspires me and when I travel I make it a point to cook with people in their homes. I believe in cooking from the heart and soul, which you can only learn from people cooking in their own kitchens.

Mediterranean cuisine refers to the culinary trends shared by a diverse array of people who live in the region around the Mediterranean Sea. The most universally used ingredient here is olive oil. Fresh vegetables dominate with a wide variety taking centrestage in dishes throughout the region. While there is some cultural variation, eggplant, artichokes, squash, tomatoes, legumes, onions, mushrooms, okra, cucumbers, and an assortment of greens and lettuces, all flourish in this region and are commonly used. Vegetables appear in dishes in a variety of forms: baked, roasted, sautéed grilled, puréed, and served fresh in salads. Meat in most of the Mediterranean recipes tends to be grilled.

The Mediterranean is divided into three culinary regions: Eastern Mediterranean, Southern Europe, and North Africa.

Eastern Mediterranean cuisine, which encompasses some Middle Eastern cuisine, describes the culinary traditions of Greece, Turkey, Syria, Lebanon, Israel, Palestine, and Egypt. Yogurt and fresh cheeses like feta, halumi, and labneh feature prominently. The flavours of parsley, sumac, mint, and lemon juice dominate the cooking palate.

Southern European cuisine, especially of Italy, southern France, and Spain has specific ingredients that distinguish it from the rest of Europe's cooking traditions. Tomatoes, garlic, capers, anchovies, mustard, anise, and pine nuts are used in a variety of combinations to flavour food. A multitude of different grains and leavened breads, pasta, and rice are staples of the region.

North African cuisine is characterized by an abundant use of spices. Cooking traditions of Morocco, Algeria, Tunisia, and Libya use cumin, coriander, saffron, cinnamon, cloves, chillies, and paprika. Harissa and ras el hanout are two fiery spice mixtures used predominantly in Moroccan cuisine, giving a characteristic heat to stews and sauces. The Moroccan tagine, a slow-cooked stew of meat, vegetables, and sauce prepared in a conical-shaped ceramic pot, is perhaps the most recognizable and popularized of dishes – aromatic, hearty, and well-balanced.

As a chef, I am extremely excited to collaborate with Foodhall for this book.

I think Foodhall has made cooking easy for professionals as well as for people cooking at home due to easy availability of ingredients and the variety of ingredients that they have! Be it the most exotic of fruits and vegetables, to cheese, to sauces, to meats, to ready mixes, to kitchen equipment, and small tools – Foodhall is the one stop destination for everything! Each and every ingredient in every recipe is easily available at Foodhall.

Hope that all of you have fun cooking with these recipes! Bon Appétit.

— Sabyasachi Gorai

Foodhall

PANTRY STAPLES

Essential ingredients you need
for these recipes.

- ACTIVE DRY YEAST
- ALLSPICE POWDER
- BEETROOT CRESS
- BLACK ORGANIC RICE
- BRINED GRAPE VINE LEAVES
- CARAWAY SEEDS
- DRIED BARBERRIES
- FALAFEL
- FETA CHEESE
- GREEK YOGURT
- HARISSA SPICE MIX
- HUMMUS
- IRANIAN LIME POWDER
- LEBANESE CUCUMBER
- PEARL COUSCOUS
- PITA BREAD
- PITA CHIPS
- POMEGRANATE MOLASSES
- RAS EL HANOUT SPICE
- RED WINE VINEGAR
- RISOTTO RICE
- ROMAINE LETTUCE
- SHAWARMA SPICE MIX
- SUMAC POWDER
- TAHINI
- YELLOW PLUM TOMATOES

Classical Greek Salad Dressed with Lemon, Olive Oil and Sumac

Fresh and colourful classic Greek salad served with a tangy dressing made of sumac, lemon and olive oil.

Preparation time: 15 minutes · Cooking time: 5 minutes · Serves: 2

ingredients

1 head romaine lettuce, washed, dried, torn into smaller bits
3 red baby onions, cut
1 Lebanese cucumber, cut
1 red bell pepper, cut
1 yellow bell pepper, cut
1 capsicum, cut
5 yellow plum tomatoes, halved
5 cherry tomatoes, halved
10 black olives, pitted
½ cup / 125 gm feta cheese, crumbled
A handful beetroot cress

For the dressing:

1 tbsp / 15 ml extra virgin olive oil
1 tsp / 5 gm Arqa sumac powder
Lemon juice to taste
Coarse sea salt to taste
Black peppercorns, freshly ground, to taste

method

1. **For the dressing**, using a hand blender, blend together the olive oil, sumac powder, lemon juice, sea salt and black pepper.
2. In a large salad bowl, combine the lettuce, onions, cucumber, red and yellow peppers, capsicum, cherry tomatoes, black olives and feta cheese. Garnish with beetroot cress.
3. Serve either with the dressing by the side or toss the salad with the dressing and then serve.

Mezze Platter Served with Pita Chips

A spread of appetizers or small bites which is a must for all Mediterranean feasts. A popular Middle Eastern mezze includes tzatziki, babaganoush, hummus, muhammara and toum along with pita chips, olives and pickled vegetables.

Preparation time: 45 minutes | Cooking time: 30 minutes | Serves: 2 (each portion serves 2)

Tzatziki

Greek sauce served with grilled meats or as a dip. Made of strained yogurt mixed with cucumber, garlic, salt, olive oil, vinegar and dill.

ingredients

½ Lebanese cucumber, grated
1 cup / 250 gm Greek yogurt
3 cloves garlic, finely chopped
2 tbsp / 30 ml extra virgin olive oil
1 tbsp / 15 ml vinegar
Coarse sea salt to taste
1 tsp / 5 gm fresh dill, finely chopped

method

1. Drain the grated cucumber through a fine mesh sieve. Keep overnight in the fridge.
2. Combine the yogurt, garlic, oil, vinegar and salt in a large bowl. Cover and refrigerate overnight.
3. Mix the drained cucumber and fresh dill with the yogurt mixture; serve.

Babaganoush

Eggplant mixed with onions, tomatoes, olive oil and various seasonings.

ingredients

1 large eggplant
4 tbsp / 60 gm tahini
3 cloves garlic, finely chopped
4 tbsp / 60 ml lemon juice
¼ tsp Arqa cumin powder
¼ cup / 60 gm red and yellow bell peppers, chopped
1 tbsp / 15 gm fresh flat-leaf parsley, finely chopped
3 tbsp / 45 ml extra virgin olive oil
Coarse sea salt to taste

method

1. Preheat the oven to 180°C / 350°F.
2. Prick the eggplant with a fork in several places, place on a tray and bake until very soft for about 25-30 minutes.
3. Remove the tray from the oven, let the eggplant cool slightly. Peel off and discard the skin.
4. Place the eggplant flesh in a blender and blend roughly. Transfer into a bowl. Add the tahini, garlic, lemon juice, cumin powder, bell peppers, parsley and olive oil; mix well. Add more salt and lemon juice, if required.
5. Drizzle some olive oil before serving.

Hummus

Creamy spread made from cooked and mashed chickpeas, blended with tahini, olive oil, lemon juice, salt and garlic.

ingredients

½ cup / 125 gm chickpeas from Traditions by Foodhall, soaked overnight
½ tbsp / 8 ml lemon juice
1 clove garlic
Coarse sea salt to taste
1 tsp / 5 gm tahini
2 tbsp / 30 ml extra virgin olive oil

method

1. Boil the chickpeas till soft. Strain and reserve the water. Allow the chickpeas to cool.
2. When cool, combine the chickpeas with lemon juice, garlic and salt in a food processor; blend to a fine purée.
3. Add the tahini and olive oil, a little at a time, and blend into a fine purée.
4. Add more salt, tahini and lemon juice, if required.

Muhammara

Walnuts and hot pepper dip originally from Aleppo, Syria.

ingredients

4 red bell peppers, roasted
4 cloves garlic, minced
½ cup / 125 gm bread crumbs, fresh
¼ cup / 60 gm Bustaan walnuts, toasted, chopped
1 tbsp / 15 ml lemon juice
2 tsp / 10 gm pomegranate molasses
1 tsp / 5 gm Arqa cumin powder
½ tsp / 2½ gm Arqa red chilli flakes
Coarse sea salt to taste
5 tbsp / 75 ml extra virgin olive oil

method

1. In a food processor, blend red bell peppers, garlic, bread crumbs, walnuts, lemon juice, pomegranate molasses, cumin, red chilli flakes and sea salt except oil until smooth. While the motor is running, add the oil gradually.
2. Serve as required.

Toum

A traditional Lebanese garlic dipping sauce.

ingredients

10-12 cloves garlic, peeled, roughly chopped
1 tsp / 5 gm coarse sea salt
1 tbsp / 15 ml lemon juice
¾ cup / 185 ml vegetable oil
2 tbsp / 30 ml water

method

1. Blend the garlic in a blender with salt and lemon juice for 2-3 minutes or until smooth. Scrape down the sides from time to time to make sure there are no chunks.
2. Add the oil, very slowly and gradually. Mix, ensuring that it is fully absorbed after each addition. Finally, add water.

Falafel Served with Hummus and Pita Bread

Lebanese-style golden fried chickpea dumplings, crisp on the outside and soft on the inside, made with fresh herbs and spices.

Preparation time: 1½ hour   Cooking time: 20 minutes   Serves: 2

ingredients

Falafel mix

OR

For the falafel:

1 cup / 250 gm chickpeas from Traditions by Foodhall, soaked overnight, strained
1 small onion, chopped
3-5 cloves garlic, finely chopped
1 small bunch fresh parsley
1 small bunch fresh green coriander
2 green chillies, finely chopped
1½ tbsp / 25 gm refined flour
Coarse sea salt to taste
1 tsp / 5 gm Arqa cumin powder, roasted
1 tsp / 5 gm Arqa coriander powder
Vegetable oil for frying

For the pita bread:

3 cups / 750 gm whole wheat flour
1¼ cups / 300 ml warm water
1 tbsp / 15 gm sugar
½ tbsp / 8 gm active dry yeast
½ tbsp / 8 gm coarse sea salt
1 tbsp / 15 ml olive oil

method

1. **For the falafel**, blend the chickpeas in a food processor along with the onion, garlic, parsley, green coriander, green chillies, flour, salt, cumin powder and coriander powder till it resembles a coarse mixture. Stir the mixture with a fork to make it even and divide it equally into small portions and shape into round balls or slider-shaped patties with wet hands. Heat the oil in a frying pan on medium heat; deep-fry the patties, in batches of 5-6, till golden brown on both sides. Remove and drain the excess oil on absorbent kitchen paper towels. Keep aside.

2. **For the pita bread**, pour ½ cup warm water in a small bowl. Stir in the sugar and yeast. Keep aside for 10-15 minutes at room temperature. In a large bowl, mix the remaining warm water with the whole wheat flour. Add the salt and olive oil; mix with a wooden spoon. After the yeast has frothed, mix it with the wheat flour and knead into a soft and smooth dough. Keep it in a greased container with some olive oil applied all over it. Cover with a kitchen towel and leave for 1-1½ hours at room temperature. Preheat the oven to 200°C / 390°F. Once the dough has doubled up, put it on a working surface and deflate it gently. Divide the dough equally into medium-sized balls and roll each out into a 6 inch-diameter disc with ¼ inch thickness. Cover them loosely with a kitchen towel and let them rest at room temperature for 10 minutes.

3. **For baking**, place the discs on a greased tray and bake at 200°C / 390°F (if baking in convection mode of microwave oven). If using a regular oven, then preheat as well as bake at 250°C / 480°F for 7-10 minutes or till puffed up and lightly browned. Bake all the pita breads this way. Serve the falafel hot along with pita bread and hummus (see recipe on pg. 126).

Harissa Spiced Potato Wedges Served with Bravas Sauce

Potato wedges seasoned with sumac and harissa spice and served with the classic bravas sauce. This recipe is a twist on the Spanish recipe of patatas bravas.

Preparation time: 20 minutes   Cooking time: 10 minutes   Serves: 2

ingredients

For the potato wedges:

3 potatoes, washed, cleaned, peeled, cut into 24 wedges
Vegetable / olive oil for frying
1 tbsp / 15 gm Arqa sumac powder
1 tbsp / 15 gm harissa spice mix (see recipe)
Coarse sea salt to taste

For the bravas sauce:

1 tbsp / 15 ml olive oil
1 clove garlic, finely chopped
1 onion, chopped
4 tomatoes, peeled, deseeded, chopped
2 red bell peppers, chopped
½ tsp / 2½ gm Arqa cayenne pepper powder

For the harissa spice mix:

½ cup / 125 gm Arqa dried red chillies, broken, seeds discarded, soaked in boiling water for 30 minutes until soft
2 cloves garlic, peeled, crushed with salt
½ tsp / 2½ gm coarse sea salt
½ tsp / 2½ gm Arqa cumin seeds, ground
1 tsp / 5 gm Arqa caraway seeds, ground
2 tbsp / 30 ml olive oil

method

1. **For the potato wedges**, par boil the potato wedges in boiling water for 2 minutes. Drain and cool on absorbent kitchen paper towels. Heat the oil in a frying pan; fry the potato wedges until golden and crisp. Remove and drain the excess oil.
2. **For the bravas sauce**, heat the olive oil in a pan; sauté the garlic and onion on low heat for 2-3 minutes or till the onion is soft and tender. Add the tomatoes, red bell peppers and cayenne pepper powder. Increase heat to medium and cook till the mix is reduced to ²/₃rd and becomes deep red in colour, for about 20 minutes. Remove from heat.
3. **For the harissa spice mix**, drain the chillies and pound or process with the crushed garlic, sea salt, ground cumin and caraway seeds. Add the olive oil to lubricate the mixture. Store in a jar and use as required.
4. Season the potato wedges with sumac powder, harissa spice and coarse sea salt.
5. Serve garnished with rosemary sprigs, accompanied with the bravas sauce for dipping.

Labneh Stuffed Lentil Kibbeh Served with Mango Chilli Dressing

The crisp lentil kibbeh with soft labneh (mint-flavoured hung yogurt) oozing out from the centre makes for a delicious vegetarian party snack. This is a vegetarian version of the famous lamb kibbeh stuffed with labneh.

Preparation time: 45 minutes | Cooking time: 10 minutes | Serves: 2

ingredients

For the lentil kibbeh:

1 cup / 250 gm split Bengal gram (*chana dal*) from Traditions by Foodhall
½ tsp / 2½ gm Arqa turmeric powder
Coarse sea salt to taste
1 small onion, chopped
1 tsp / 5 gm Arqa cumin powder
½ tsp / 2½ gm Arqa coriander powder
A few sprigs fresh green coriander
½ cup / 125 gm bread crumbs
Vegetable oil for frying

For the labneh:

1 cup / 250 gm hung yogurt
½ tsp / 2½ gm fresh mint leaves, chopped

For the mango chilli dressing:

3 tbsp / 45 gm mango purée
½ tsp / 2½ gm Arqa red chilli powder
1 tsp / 5 ml vinegar
2 tbsp / 30 ml olive oil
Coarse sea salt to taste

method

1. **For the lentil kibbeh**, boil the Bengal gram with turmeric powder and salt. Strain the dal once cooked and grind in a food processor along with onion, cumin powder, coriander powder, sea salt, green coriander and bread crumbs to form a dough-like mix.
2. **For the labneh**, mix the hung yogurt with the mint leaves. Keep aside.
3. Divide the lentil dough equally into medium-sized balls. With your thumb make a depression in the centre and stuff each dough ball with about 1 tbsp labneh; sealing the filling inside.
4. Shape the balls carefully so that they are flat from the bottom and conical from the top. Place on a greased plate.
5. **For the mango chilli dressing**, blend the mango purée, red chilli powder, vinegar, olive oil and sea salt in a mixer to a smooth purée.
6. Heat the oil in a pan; deep-fry the kibbeh till golden brown. Remove and drain the excess oil on absorbent kitchen paper towels. Repeat till all are fried.
7. Serve hot along with the mango chilli dressing.

Labneh Two Way Served with Tender Asparagus Spears and Roasted Vegetables

Labneh balls marinated in chilli oil and served with blanched asparagus and pita chips – the chef's signature dish.

Preparation time: 45 minutes + overnight for marination | Cooking time: 3-4 minutes | Serves: 2

ingredients

1 pc pita bread (see recipe on pg. 128)
3 asparagus, blanched in salted water for 2 minutes
½ cup / 125 gm hung yogurt
2 tsp / 10 gm Arqa star anise powder
Coarse sea salt and black pepper to taste
1 cup / 250 ml chilli oil
1 tsp / 5 ml olive oil
½ onion, sliced
½ red bell pepper, roasted
½ yellow bell pepper, roasted
1 tbsp / 15 gm Arqa sumac powder

method

1. Mix the hung yogurt with the star anise powder, sea salt and pepper. Prepare 2 balls (30 gm each) of the hung yogurt and marinate them overnight in a bowl of chilli oil.
2. Cut the pita bread into pieces and dry them in the oven at low temperature to prepare chips. Remove and keep aside.
3. Heat the olive oil in a skillet; sauté the onion, red and yellow bell peppers. Season with salt and pepper. Remove and arrange in a dip bowl.
4. In a separate dip bowl, put one labneh ball. Roll the other labneh ball in sumac powder and put in another dip bowl.
5. Arrange and serve the asparagus sticks, pita bread chips, sautéed onion and bell pepper and both the labneh balls on a platter.

Vine Leaves Dolmas Dressed with Extra Virgin Olive Oil and Coarse Sea Salt

Brined grape vine steamed leaves stuffed with raw rice and aromatic herbs – a traditional Turkish recipe.

Preparation time: 1 hour   Cooking time: 30 minutes   Serves: 2

ingredients

30 brined grape vine leaves
½ cup / 125 ml olive oil

For the stuffing:

½ cup / 125 gm rice, washed, soaked for an hour
1 onion, chopped
1 tomato, chopped
4-5 sprigs fresh parsley, chopped
1 tsp / 5 gm Arqa allspice powder
1 tbsp / 15 gm currants, chopped
1 tsp / 5 gm sugar
2 tbsp / 30 ml lemon juice
Coarse sea salt to taste
Black peppercorns, freshly ground, to taste

For the base:

1 carrot
1 tbsp / 15 gm celery, roughly chopped
2 onions

method

1. **For the stuffing**, mix together the rice, onion, tomato, parsley, allspice powder, currants, sugar, lemon juice, sea salt and black pepper. Keep aside.
2. **For the grape vine leaves**, take one leaf at a time and prepare it to be stuffed by cutting off the hard stem and spreading it out flat on a clear, preferably glass surface area, with the stem end pointing towards you.
3. Put ½ tbsp stuffing as wide and long as your little finger alongside the bottom of the leaf, in front of you, horizontally. Flip close the right and left hand side of the leaf over the stuffing and roll, rather tightly, but without too much pressure. Be careful not to tear them. Repeat till all are done.
4. **For the base**, place the carrot, celery and onions to form a bed at the bottom of a deep pot; add enough water to cover the vegetables. Now spread a layer of vine leaves over the vegetables.
5. One by one, place the rolled dolmas next to each other. Continue lining up the pieces above the first layer until all the dolmas are in the pot.
6. Cook on low heat until the dolmas are done, which is when the rice inside is cooked and the leaves are softer. This will take about 20-30 minutes.
7. Serve on a platter dressed with extra virgin olive oil and sea salt.

Sweet and Sour Green Eggplant Served with Tamarind Glaze and Walnuts

Crispy fried green eggplants garnished with nutty walnuts and accompanied with sweet and tangy tamarind glaze.

Preparation time: 20 minutes Cooking time: 10 minutes Serves: 2

ingredients

2 green eggplants, small, halved lengthwise
Salt and black pepper to taste
Vegetable oil for frying
1 tbsp / 15 gm tamarind paste
2 tsp / 10 gm sugar
½ tbsp / 8 ml olive oil
½ cup / 125 gm Bustaan walnuts, roasted, chopped
4 Arqa red chillies, fried
A few sprigs fresh parsley

method

1. Sprinkle salt and pepper over the eggplants and keep aside.
2. Heat the oil in a pan; fry the eggplants on medium heat, until crisp and golden. Remove and drain the excess oil on absorbent kitchen paper towels.
3. Blend together the tamarind paste, sugar, olive oil, salt and pepper to make a glaze.
4. In a platter, arrange the fried eggplants and garnish with walnuts. Serve with the tamarind dressing on the side topped with fried red chillies and parsley.

Spanakopitas Served with Barberry Compote

Buttery and savoury parcels filled with spinach and feta cheese served with a spiced barberry compote.

Preparation time: 35 minutes | Cooking time: 45 minutes | Serves: 2

ingredients

For the spanakopitas:
10 sheets phyllo pastry leaves
1 bundle fresh spinach, cleaned, de-stemmed
1 cup / 250 gm feta cheese
Coarse sea salt and black pepper to taste
1 tbsp / 15 ml vegetable oil

For the barberry compote:
2 cups / 500 gm dried barberries
1 cup / 250 gm sugar
½ cup / 125 ml honey
3 Arqa cardamom pods
2 Arqa cloves
1 Arqa star anise
1 sprig thyme
1 Arqa bay leaf
Coarse sea salt to taste

method

1. **For the spanakopitas**, preheat the oven to 180°C / 350°F. Blanch the spinach, strain and chop. Mix with the feta cheese and season with salt and pepper to prepare the stuffing. Lay out a phyllo sheet and brush with butter. Repeat with the other sheets. Put 3 tbsp of the prepared spinach mixture in the centre of each sheet and wrap into a parcel. Lightly brush 4 muffin moulds with oil and place the parcels in them carefully taking the shape of the mould. Bake uncovered for 45 minutes or until golden-brown and crisp.
2. **For the barberry compote**, in a medium-sized saucepan, combine the barberries with the sugar and honey. Put the cardamom pods, cloves, star anise, thyme sprigs and bay leaf in a double layer of cheesecloth and tie them into a bundle. Add the bundle to the saucepan and bring to the boil. Cover and simmer on moderately low heat until the berries are softened and the sugar has melted, about 10 minutes. Season lightly with salt. Remove the pan from the heat and keep aside to cool.
3. Discard the spice bundle. Add half of the barberries and juices to the food processor and purée. Return the purée to the saucepan and season the barberry compote lightly with salt.
4. Serve the spanakopitas with the barberry compote.

Fish served with Pistachios, Onions and Pomegranate Salad Flavoured with Olive Oil, Lemon and Dill Dressing

A sweet and nutty salad with plenty of crunch and flavours accompanied with pan-fried fish.

Preparation time: 30 minutes | Cooking time: 5 minutes | Serves: 2

ingredients

5 pcs / 40 gm each mackerel fish, boneless, cut into chunks, cleaned, pat-dried with kitchen towel
3 tbsp / 45 ml olive oil
1 tbsp / 15 ml lemon juice
2 cloves garlic, puréed
A few sprigs fresh dill leaves
Coarse sea salt to taste
Vegetable oil for frying

For the salad dressing:
2 tbsp / 30 ml extra virgin olive oil
1 tbsp / 15 ml lemon juice
A few sprigs fresh dill, finely chopped
Coarse sea salt and black pepper, freshly ground, to taste

For the salad:
10-12 arugula leaves
3 tbsp / 45 gm fresh flat-leaf parsley, roughly chopped
1 onion, thinly sliced
¼ cup / 60 gm Bustaan pistachios
1 pomegranate

method

1. Marinate the fish with olive oil, lemon juice, garlic purée, dill leaves and coarse sea salt. Cover and refrigerate for 30 minutes.
2. Heat the oil in a skillet; pan-fry the fish on both sides for a minute each. Remove and keep aside.
3. **For the salad dressing**, in a bowl, blend the olive oil, lemon juice, fresh dill (reserve some for garnishing), salt and black pepper with a hand blender.
4. **For the salad**, in a bowl, combine together the arugula, parsley, onion and pistachios (reserve some for garnishing). Toss the ingredients with the dressing.
5. On a plate, arrange the salad and the pan-fried fish garnished with some pistachios, pomegranate seeds and fresh dill leaves.

Prawn Saganaki Served with Iranian Lime Pearl Couscous

Melt-in-the mouth delicious jumbo prawns simmered in tomato sauce, topped with feta cheese and served with couscous pilaf.

Preparation time: 15 minutes   Cooking time: 30 minutes   Serves: 2

ingredients

For the prawn saganaki:
6 jumbo prawns, with shell
3 tbsp / 45 ml olive oil
1 onion, sliced
4 cloves garlic, sliced
½ cup / 125 ml white wine
5 tomatoes, chopped
2 tbsp / 30 gm tomato paste
½ cup / 125 ml prawn / shrimp stock
2 tbsp / 30 gm parsley, chopped
Salt and black pepper to taste
5 tbsp / 75 gm feta cheese, crumbled
5 black olives

For the Iranian lime couscous pilaf:
1 cup / 250 gm pearl couscous
1 tsp / 5 gm Arqa Iranian lime powder
2 tbsp / 30 ml red chilli oil
Coarse sea salt and black pepper to taste
1 tbsp / 15 gm pomegranate seeds

method

1. **For the prawn saganaki**, heat the oil in a skillet and sauté the onion till translucent. Add the garlic and sauté for another minute. Add the white wine, chopped tomatoes, tomato paste, prawn / shrimp stock and 1 tbsp parsley; simmer for 10 minutes or till the mix is reduced to half. Stir in the prawns and cook for 3-5 minutes. Season with salt and pepper. Remove the skillet from the heat, add the feta cheese and garnish with black olives and remaining parsley. Keep aside.
2. **For the Iranian lime couscous pilaf**, boil the pearl couscous for 10-12 minutes; sieve into a pot and leave covered for 5 minutes. Then add the Iranian lime powder, red chilli oil, salt and pepper; mix thoroughly.
3. Serve in a bowl garnished with pomegranate seeds and accompanied with prawn saganaki.

Sumac Rubbed Pollo Ala Plancha

A flavourful, rustic Spanish dish made of succulent chicken thighs, whole spices, chilli and fresh herbs, cooked in a cast iron pan (plancha).

Preparation time: 1 hour 15 minutes | Cooking time: 10 minutes | Serves: 2

ingredients

5 pcs / 40 gm each chicken thighs, boneless
½ cup / 120 ml olive oil
1 tbsp / 15 gm Arqa sumac powder
Coarse sea salt to taste
A few sprigs rosemary
5 Arqa star anise
5 baby onions, oven roasted
5 cherry tomatoes
5 green olives
5 black olives
5 cloves garlic, roasted
5 Arqa whole red chillies
5-6 fresh basil leaves, torn by hand
Coarse sea salt and black pepper to taste
1 tbsp / 15 ml red wine vinegar
A few sprigs fresh parsley

method

1. Marinate the chicken thighs with ¼ cup olive oil, sumac powder and sea salt. Refrigerate for an hour.
2. Heat ¼ cup oil in a cast-iron pan; add the rosemary sprigs and sear the chicken thighs on both sides. Add the star anise, baby onions, cherry tomatoes, green olives, black olives, roasted garlic cloves, whole red chillies and basil; cook for a minute. Season with sea salt and black pepper.
3. Add the red wine vinegar to the pan to deglaze all the flavours. Cook till the chicken is tender. Add more seasoning, if required.
4. Serve hot in the cast-iron pan itself garnished with fresh parsley leaves.

Chicken and Sausage Paella with Black and White Rice

Wholesome chicken paella with a combination of risotto and organic black rice.

Preparation time: 20 minutes | Cooking time: 35 minutes | Serves: 2

ingredients

5 pcs / 30 gm each chicken dices
10 chicken sausages, whole
2 cups / 500 ml chicken stock
¼ tsp Arqa saffron
2 tbsp / 30 ml olive oil
1 onion, finely chopped
1 cup / 250 gm arborio rice from Traditions by Foodhall
2 tbsp / 30 ml white wine
1 cup / 250 gm black organic rice from Traditions by Foodhall, soaked overnight
1 tsp / 5 gm Arqa sweet paprika powder
½ capsicum, cut into batons
½ red bell pepper, cut into batons
½ yellow bell pepper, cut into batons
2 cloves garlic, crushed
Salt and black pepper to taste
1 lemon, cut into wedges
A few sprigs fresh parsley

method

1. Combine the chicken stock and saffron in a medium-sized saucepan. Cover with a tight-fitting lid and bring to the boil on high heat. Reduce heat to low and simmer gently.
2. Heat 1 tbsp oil in another pan on low heat; add the onion and sauté till translucent and soft.
3. Add the arborio rice and cook till translucent. After a minute, add the white wine and keep stirring till it evaporates.
4. Once the wine is absorbed by the rice, add a ladleful of hot stock and a good pinch of salt. Mix in the black rice, reduce heat to low and simmer so that the rice doesn't cook too quickly on the outside.
5. Keep adding stock, stirring and almost massaging the creamy starch out of the rice, allowing each ladleful to be absorbed before adding the next. This will take around 15 minutes. Taste the rice and add paprika; continue to add stock until the rice is soft but with a slight bite.
6. Heat 1 tbsp oil in a flat/paella pan on medium heat; cook the diced chicken and sausages, stirring for 4-5 minutes or until brown. Add the capsicum, red and yellow bell peppers and garlic; stir for 2 minutes. Add the cooked rice and sweet paprika. Cook for a minute, stirring to combine.
7. Serve in the paella pan garnished with lemon wedges and parsley.

Chicken Shawarma, Freshly Baked Pita, Lebanese Pickles, Hummus and Potato Wedges

Tender chicken marinated in Mediterranean spices, wrapped with colourful peppers, pickled vegetables, potato wedges and creamy hummus.

Preparation time: 1 hour | Cooking time: 20 minutes | Serves: 2

ingredients

5 pcs / 40 gm each chicken thighs, boneless
1½ tbsp / 25 ml olive oil
Juice of one lemon
1 tbsp / 15 gm Arqa shawarma spice mix (or see recipe)
Coarse sea salt to taste
Vegetable oil for frying
1 tsp / 5 ml red wine vinegar
1 yellow bell pepper, cut into strips
½ red bell peppers, cut into strips
½ capsicum, cut into strips
8-10 potato wedges (see recipe on pg. 130)
2 pita breads (see recipe on pg. 128)
4 tbsp / 60 gm hummus (see recipe on pg. 126)
½ cup / 125 gm mukhalal (pickled vegetables, see recipe on pg. 154)

For the shawarma spice mix recipe:
2 tbsp / 30 gm hung yogurt
1 tsp / 5 gm tomato paste
1 tbsp / 15 gm Arqa cumin powder
1 tbsp / 15 gm Arqa coriander powder
1 tbsp / 15 gm Arqa garlic powder
½ tbsp / 8 gm Arqa paprika
1 tsp / 5 gm Arqa turmeric powder
½ tsp / 2½ gm Arqa cloves, ground
½ tsp / 2½ gm Arqa cayenne pepper, ground
1 tsp / 5 gm black pepper, ground
½ tsp / 2½ gm Arqa cinnamon, ground

method

1. Marinate the chicken thighs with olive oil, lemon juice, shawarma spice mix and salt. Refrigerate for an hour.
2. **For the shawarma spice mix**, in a mixing bowl, combine the hung yogurt and tomato paste with the cumin powder, coriander powder, garlic powder, paprika, turmeric powder, ground clove, cayenne pepper, black pepper and cinnamon. Mix and store in an airtight container or bottle. Use as required.
3. Heat the oil in a skillet; pan-fry the chicken on both sides for about 5-7 minutes or until well done.
4. Add the red wine vinegar to deglaze the pan. Remove the pan from the heat and let the chicken rest.
5. In a separate pan, stir-fry the yellow and red bell peppers and capsicum in little oil and season with salt.
6. Fry the potato wedges and remove and drain the excess oil on absorbent kitchen paper towels.
7. Take a pita bread, spread 2 tbsp hummus evenly on top. Arrange the mukhalal vegetables, chicken, stir-fried bell peppers and potato wedges on top. Serve wrapped or as it is.

Lamb Tagine with Root Vegetables, Tagine Spice, Tomato and Pepper Gravy

Amazingly aromatic traditional Moroccan slow-cooked lamb stew with a burst of flavours.

Preparation time: 15 minutes Cooking time: 35 minutes Serves: 2

ingredients

4 back strap lamb, with 3 ribs each
1 Arqa bay leaf
1 Arqa mace
8 black peppercorns
1 tbsp / 15 gm Arqa ras el hanout spice mix (or see recipe)

For the ras el hanout spice mix:
2½ tbsp / 35 gm Arqa cumin seeds
2 tbsp / 30 gm Arqa coriander seeds
1 tbsp / 15 gm Arqa cinnamon, ground
2 tsp / 10 gm dry ginger, ground
2 tsp / 10 gm black peppercorns
1 tsp / 5 gm Arqa turmeric, ground
½ tsp / 2½ gm Arqa cardamom powder
A pinch of Arqa saffron

For the gravy:
1 tbsp / 15 ml olive oil
5 cloves garlic, pounded
3 Arqa star anise
4 Arqa whole red chillies
1 tsp / 5 gm Arqa fennel powder
1 tsp / 5 gm Arqa coriander powder
1 Arqa bay leaf
1 tsp / 5 gm Arqa Kashmiri chilli powder
2 cups / 500 gm tomatoes, peeled, deseeded
4 carrots, peeled, cut into batons
10 baby onions, peeled
1 cauliflower, cut into florets
¼ cup / 60 gm red currants
Coarse sea salt and black pepper to taste
A few fresh parsley leaves, for garnishing
1 tbsp / 15 gm Bustaan pistachios, chopped

method

1. Pressure cook the lamb with the whole spices (bay leaf, mace and black peppercorns) and ras el hanout spice mix till tender and off the bone. Separate the pieces and sieve and reserve the stock.

2. **For the ras el hanout spice mix**, toast the cumin seeds, coriander seeds, cinnamon, ginger and black peppercorns in a small pan until aromatic and have turned a shade or two darker. This step is important and should not be skipped as it enhances the flavours. Grind the spices in a spice grinder or in a mortar and pestle, then add the turmeric and cardamom powders and saffron, crush to a fine powder. Store in a sealed jar for up to 6 months and use as required.

3. **For the gravy**, heat the olive oil in a pan; sauté the garlic with the star anise. Temper the whole red chillies, fennel powder, coriander powder, bay leaf and Kashmiri chilli powder. Add the tomatoes and lamb stock and cook on medium heat for 15-20 minutes, stirring occasionally. Add the lamb pieces, carrots, baby onions, cauliflower and red currants; stir well. Simmer, covered for 10-15 minutes.

4. Season with salt and pepper to taste.

5. Serve in a tagine bowl garnished with parsley and pistachios.

Chef's Tip: *You may also slow cook the lamb instead of using pressure cooker.*

Mukhalal

Traditional Lebanese pickled vegetables used as an accompaniment to a mezze platter, snacks and wraps.

Preparation time: 15 minutes Cooking time: 10 minutes + 12 hours of overnight refrigeration Makes: 1 jar

ingredients

2 cucumbers, cut
2 radishes, cut
2 beetroots, cut
1¼ cups / 300 ml water, boiled
10 tbsp / 150 ml red wine vinegar / white vinegar
Salt to taste
2 tbsp / 30 gm sugar
2 green chillies

method

1. In a big bowl, combine the cucumbers, radishes, beetroots, boiled water, vinegar, salt and sugar; stir to prepare a pickling solution.
2. Place the vegetable mix along with the green chillies into a jar. Pack tightly.
3. Pour the pickling solution over the vegetables to cover completely.
4. Cover tightly with a lid and pickle in the jar overnight (for best results).
5. Serve along with snacks, pita bread and various mezze dips.

DESSERTS

by POOJA DHINGRA

When I started my patisserie in 2010, a lot of my time was spent educating the customers. Our menu had to balance simpler, familiar flavours with slightly more sophisticated ones. Today, seven years later, I find that I can experiment as much as I like, and people cannot seem to get enough. Whether its matcha or baklava or choux pastry, the Indian palate has evolved enough to embrace the world on a plate. A lot of this, of course, has to do with travel and popular culture but it is also fuelled by the easy availability of exotic ingredients.

In major Indian cities, and several tier-2 ones as well, walking into a store like Foodhall exposes you to a range of cultures and cuisines. When I walk around buying ingredients, I love to try new things and appreciate that there are a lot of tasting plates; the staff, too, are educated and helpful. As a foodie myself, this is wonderful but it's even more wonderful for me as a chef.

The recipes I like to bake all have a personal story and are my food memories that translate into a product. For this book I've tried to use a mix of some of my happiest memories, most of them are related to travel. The Kesar Pista cupcakes are reminiscent of Diwali in my house. With the spiced macarons, I add my own touch to a very traditional French technique. The Dark Chocolate Fondant is my favourite and the easiest to make. I made the mistake of telling my brother how easy it was, and now when he has a chocolate craving he demands that I make it for him. Delicate flavours like rose petal and spices such as cardamom and cinnamon are frequently used in Indian desserts. In many of my recipes in the book I hope to present familiar Indian spices and nuts in a whole new and more modern avatar.

The thing to remember while baking is to be prepared. Get a good weighing scale and the best quality of ingredients you can find. Once you get comfortable with these recipes, try and experiment with the flavours to make them your own! I hope you enjoy baking with them as much as I've enjoyed creating them. Happy baking J

— Pooja Dhingra

Foodhall

PANTRY STAPLES

Essential ingredients you need
for these recipes.

- ALMOND POWDER
- BAKING SODA
- CASTER SUGAR
- CHIA SEEDS
- CHOCOLATE SPRINKLES
- COCOA POWDER
- CONDENSED MILK
- CORNSTARCH
- DARK CHOCOLATE
- DRIED ROSE PETALS
- EARL GREY TEA
- GELATIN
- HAZELNUTS
- KIWI
- MASCARPONE CHEESE
- MATCH POWDER
- PHILADELPHIA CREAM CHEESE
- RASPBERRY JAM
- ROSE ESSENCE
- ROSE SYRUP
- SAFFRON
- VANILLA BEAN
- WASABI PASTE
- WHITE CHOCOLATE

Spiced Macarons

Melt-in-the-mouth, light and airy, meringue-like French macarons with cinnamon- and ginger-flavoured ganache filling!

Preparation time: 45 minutes · Cooking time: 15 minutes · Makes: 20 macarons / 40 shells

ingredients

For the macarons:

6½ tbsp / 100 gm powdered sugar
6½ tbsp / 100 gm almond powder from Traditions by Foodhall
5 tbsp / 75 ml egg whites
¼ cup / 60 gm caster sugar
1 tsp / 5 ml liquid food colouring

For the spiced ganache:

6½ tbsp / 100 ml cream
1 tsp / 5 gm Arqa cinnamon powder
½ tsp / 2½ gm ginger, ground
½ tsp / 2½ gm Arqa cardamom powder
1¼ cups / 300 gm white chocolate, chopped

method

1. **For the macarons**, sift together the powdered sugar and almond powder so that there are no lumps. In a separate bowl, beat the egg whites until they start to froth. Then add in the caster sugar and whisk until stiff peaks are formed. Mix the stiff egg white meringue with the powdered sugar and almond mix. Add the food colouring. Use a spatula to mix till the batter flows freely. Pipe this batter over a baking tray lined with parchment paper, in circles around 1-inch wide, evenly spaced 1-inch apart. Set the tray aside for 30 minutes. Bake for 10-12 minutes at 165°C / 330°F. Allow to cool completely before removing from the baking sheet.
2. **For the spiced ganache**, heat the cream in a pan over medium heat; add the cinnamon powder, ground ginger and cardamom powder and bring to the boil. Remove the pan from the heat immediately and let the spices infuse with the cream for 10 minutes or so.
3. In the meantime, place the chopped chocolate in a stainless-steel bowl.
4. After 10 minutes, return the infused cream to the stove and simmer over medium heat. As soon as the cream is heated, strain it into the bowl of chocolate. Let it stand for 5 minutes and then stir with a whisk until smooth. Allow to cool and then refrigerate.
5. **To assemble**, pair similar-sized macaron shells together. Pipe the ganache onto one shell from each pair. Do not over fill or else it will ooze out once sandwiched. Gently press the shells together and serve.
6. For variation, one can replace the spices with any other essence or flavour as per taste.

Chef's Tip: *The trick to make perfect macarons is to weigh each ingredient correctly; even the slightest alteration will change the recipe completely. The flavour comes from the filling and not the shell. Always store in an airtight container.*

Matcha Cookies

Shortbread-like cookies flavoured with matcha powder - a perfect tea-time treat.

Preparation time: 2 hours (including resting time) Cooking time: 15 minutes Makes: 30

ingredients

13 tbsp / 200 gm butter
1 tsp / 5 gm matcha powder from The House of Tea by Foodhall
1 tsp / 5 ml vanilla essence
½ cup / 125 gm caster sugar
1 cup / 250 gm refined flour

method

1. Whisk together the butter, matcha powder and vanilla essence until smooth.
2. Add the caster sugar and whisk again till light and fluffy.
3. Fold in the flour with a spatula and knead the mixture slightly to make a dough. Place it on a sheet of cling wrap and roll into the shape of a log. Refrigerate for an hour or two, or until it is firm to touch.
4. Open the cling wrap and cut the log into medium-sized pieces. Place them on a baking tray lined with parchment paper.
5. Bake in a preheated oven at 165°C / 330°F for 15 minutes or until the edges turn brown. Remove and serve.

Earl Grey Tea Cake

A slightly dense tea cake with a moist crumb that can last for a couple of days outside the fridge.

Preparation time: 45 minutes | Cooking time: 35 minutes | Makes: 1 (6-inch cake)

ingredients

2 Earl grey tea bags from The House of Tea by Foodhall, cut open and emptied out
½ cup / 125 ml milk
6½ tbsp / 100 gm butter
1 tbsp / 15 gm caster sugar
13 tbsp / 200 gm condensed milk
½ cup / 125 gm refined flour
1 tsp / 5 gm baking powder
½ tsp / 2½ gm baking soda

method

1. In a pan, steep the tea powder in the milk and let it infuse for 10 minutes.
2. Put the pan on the heat and bring the infused milk to a gentle simmer. After 10 minutes, strain the tea and keep the milk aside.
3. Whisk together the butter and caster sugar till light and fluffy. Then add in the infused milk and condensed milk. Whisk well to combine.
4. Sift together the flour, baking powder, and baking soda. Fold this into the milk and sugar batter with a spatula.
5. Pour the cake batter into a lined 6-inch cake tin. Bake at 180°C / 355°F for 30-35 minutes or till a skewer inserted in the centre of the cake comes out clean.

Baklava Cupcakes

Extremely popular traditional sweet pastry of the imperial kitchens. A delicious crunchy crumble with soft cake.

Preparation time: 45 minutes | Cooking time: 15 minutes | Makes: 20 mini cupcakes

ingredients

For the cupcakes:

6½ tbsp / 100 gm butter
6½ tbsp / 100 gm caster sugar
1 egg
5¼ tbsp / 80 gm refined flour
Arqa dried rose petals for decoration

For the crumble:

3¼ tbsp / 50 gm butter
3¼ tbsp / 50 gm brown sugar
1 tbsp / 15 ml honey
4 tbsp / 60 gm oats
2 tbsp / 30 gm Bustaan pistachios, chopped
1 tsp / 5 ml rose syrup
½ tsp / 2½ ml rose essence

method

1. **For the crumble**, heat the butter, brown sugar and honey in a saucepan over medium heat till the butter melts. Add the oats, pistachios, rose syrup and rose essence; stir continuously till the ingredients are well incorporated and form a soft dough.
2. **For the cupcakes**, whisk the butter and caster sugar in a bowl till light and fluffy. Beat in the egg, and fold the flour in. Place liners in the cupcake moulds and pipe the cupcake batter halfway into each liner.
3. Take a small amount of the crumble mix and flatten it on your palm. Place it on top of the batter in each mould.
4. Bake at 175°C / 350°F for 15 minutes or till a skewer inserted in the centre of the cupcakes comes out clean.
5. Serve the cupcakes decorated with dried rose petals.

Kesar Pista Cupcakes

The saffron-flavoured cupcakes with pistachio frosting make a great gifting option instead of the traditional mithai *during Diwali.*

Preparation time: 50 minutes | Cooking time: 15 minutes | Makes: 24 mini cupcakes

ingredients

1-2 tsp / 5-10 gm Arqa saffron strands
5¼ tbsp / 80 ml milk
7 tbsp / 110 gm butter
13 tbsp / 200 gm caster sugar
2 eggs
10 tbsp / 150 gm refined flour
1 tsp / 5 gm baking powder

For the pistachio butter cream:
6½ tbsp / 100 gm unsalted butter
15 tbsp / 225 gm icing or powdered sugar
1 tbsp / 15 ml milk
6½ tbsp / 100 gm Bustaan pistachios, powdered
A few drops green liquid food colouring

method

1. Infuse the saffron in the milk and let it sit for 15 minutes.
2. In a bowl, beat together the butter and caster sugar till light and fluffy. Add one egg at a time, whisking after each addition to ensure it is well incorporated.
3. In a separate bowl, sift together the flour and baking powder and fold into the butter-egg mixture. Pour in the milk and mix gently to incorporate.
4. Line each mould of the cupcake tray. Pipe the batter into each liner only until three-fourth full.
5. Bake at 175°C / 350°F for 15 minutes in a preheated oven or till a skewer inserted in the centre of the cake comes out clean. Remove and allow to cool.
6. **For the pistachio butter cream**, in a bowl, whisk the butter until smooth. Gradually, add in the icing sugar and whisk well. Pour in the milk and beat to combine. Keep whisking the frosting until it is light and fluffy. Add the powdered pistachios and fold in with a spatula till fully combined. Then add in the food colouring.
7. In case you plan to use this frosting later, cover the bowl with cling wrap to prevent it from drying out.
8. Frost the cupcakes once cool enough to handle, and just before serving.

Brazilian Brigadeiros

Gooey chocolate truffle treat, a popular Brazilian candy - not only delicious and beautiful but also super simple to make.

Preparation time: 45 minutes | Cooking time: 10-15 minutes + 30 minutes refrigeration | Makes: 20 bite sized truffles

ingredients

400 gm condensed milk
1 tsp / 5 gm cocoa powder
2 tbsp / 30 gm butter
Chocolate sprinkles, as required, for rolling

method

1. Mix together the condensed milk, cocoa powder, and butter in a saucepan over medium heat. Keep stirring continuously for 10-15 minutes or till the mix becomes thick and sticky and pulls away from the bottom of the pan.
2. Pour the mix into a greased tray and allow to cool completely; around 30 minutes.
3. Divide the mixture into small portions and with greased palms shape into tablespoon-sized balls. Coat with chocolate sprinkles.
4. Refrigerate for 30 minutes before serving.

White Chocolate and Wasabi Cheesecake

No-fuss dessert with a crushed biscuit base topped with cream cheese, wasabi, and white chocolate filling. The heat from the wasabi is balanced out by the white chocolate.

Preparation time: 4-6 hours (including resting time) Cooking time: 5-7 minutes Makes: 1 (9-inch cheesecake)

ingredients

For the crust:
200 gm digestive biscuits
3¼ tbsp / 50 gm butter
3¼ tbsp / 50 gm caster sugar

For the filling:
13 tbsp / 200 gm Philadelphia cream cheese
13 tbsp / 200 gm condensed milk
6½ tbsp / 100 ml whipped cream
1 tbsp / 15 ml lemon juice
5 tbsp / 75 ml melted white chocolate
1 tsp / 5 gm wasabi paste
1¾ tbsp / 25 gm gelatin
¼ cup / 60 ml water

method

1. **For the crust**, crumble the digestive biscuits with a rolling pin or food processor. Melt the butter in a saucepan. Add the digestive biscuit crumbs and caster sugar; mix well. Remove from heat.
2. Line the base and sides of the cake tin (9-inch springform cake tin with a removable base) with the crust mixture. Use the back of a spoon to press it down well and smoothen it out.
3. Bake at 165°C / 330°F for 5-7 minutes. Allow to cool.
4. **For the filling**, whisk the cream cheese and condensed milk with a blender. In a separate bowl, beat the cream until thick. Then add it to the cream cheese mixture. Fold in the lemon juice. Gently mix in the melted chocolate and wasabi paste till properly combined.
5. Mix the gelatin with the water and heat gently, stirring all the time until the gelatin dissolves properly. Remove from heat and allow to cool. Strain it through a sieve.
6. Add the cooled gelatin in a thin stream to the mix, making sure to whisk well so that there are no lumps. Pour this into the prepared tin. Cover and refrigerate for 4-6 hours.

No-Bake Oreo Pie

A no fuss pie made of Oreo crust with a tangy cream cheese filling. A perfect treat for all cookies and cream lovers - an ideal summer dessert!

Preparation time: 20 minutes | Cooking time: 20 minutes + overnight | Makes: 1 (8-inch pie)

ingredients

For the crust:

200 gm Oreo cookies
3¼ tbsp / 50 ml melted butter
5 tsp / 25 gm caster sugar

For the filling:

15 tbsp / 225 gm Philadelphia cream cheese
Cream of Oreo cookies
6½ tbsp / 100 gm caster sugar
6½ tbsp / 100 ml whipped cream
1 tsp / 5 ml lemon juice

method

1. **For the crust**, remove the cream from the cookies and keep in a separate bowl. Crush the cookies and set 50 gm aside for the filling. Mix together 150 gm of the crushed cookies with the melted butter and caster sugar till sticky. Spread it evenly over an 8-inch springform tin. Use the back of a spoon to press it down and smoothen it out. Refrigerate for 15-20 minutes or till hard.
2. **For the filling**, whisk the cream cheese, Oreo cookie cream and caster sugar till combined. In a separate bowl, whip the cream till stiff peaks form. Fold into the cheese mix. Fold in the lemon juice and 50 gm of crushed Oreos.
3. Pour over the chilled crust and refrigerate overnight until firmly set.

Chef's Tip: *Some mint essence can be added to the filling if one feels like experimenting a little.*

Kiwi Pavlova

A sweet, crumbly meringue topped with whipped cream and tangy kiwi fruit. The acidity or sourness of the kiwi perfectly complements the sweetness of the cream and meringue.

Preparation time: 45 minutes   Cooking time: 45 minutes   Makes: 1 pavlova, Serves: 4

ingredients

2 kiwis, sliced
1 tbsp / 15 gm cornstarch
½ cup / 125 gm caster sugar
3 egg whites
1 tbsp / 15 ml white wine vinegar
1 tsp / 5 ml vanilla essence
3¼ tbsp / 50 ml whipped cream

method

1. Preheat the oven to 135°C / 275° F for 10 minutes.
2. Mix the cornstarch with the caster sugar.
3. In a medium-sized bowl, whisk the egg whites until frothy. Gradually add in the cornstarch–caster sugar mix; whisk until soft peaks form.
4. Now add the white wine vinegar and vanilla essence; whisk till the meringue is glossy.
5. Spoon the meringue onto a lined baking tray. Use the back of teaspoon to make a dent in the middle. Bake at 135°C / 275°F for 45 minutes.
6. Remove the tray from the oven and allow the meringue to cool. Fill the dent with whipped cream and kiwis.
7. Store the meringue in an airtight container until ready to eat, or else it gets soggy. For variation, replace kiwis with berries or pineapple.

Tiramisu-style Nutella Mousse

Mascarpone cheese and chocolate flavoured coffee mousse dusted with cocoa powder and chopped hazelnuts – the ultimate spin on the traditional tiramisu.

Preparation time: 30 minutes | Setting time: 6-8 hours | Serves: 2

ingredients

350 gm mascarpone cheese
2 tbsp / 30 ml strong black coffee
13 tbsp / 200 gm Nutella
6½ tbsp / 100 ml whipped cream
Cocoa powder for dusting
A few Bustaan hazelnuts, chopped, roasted, for garnishing

method

1. Whisk together the mascarpone cheese and black coffee into a smooth mixture. Add the Nutella and whisk again to make sure it is well combined.
2. In a separate bowl, beat the whipped cream till stiff peaks form. Fold into the Nutella cheese mix.
3. Pour the mousse into individual glasses or in a big bowl. Refrigerate for at least 6 hours or overnight for 8 hours.
4. Dust the mousse with some cocoa powder and serve chilled garnished with chopped hazelnuts.

Sweet Waffles with Salted Caramel Sauce

Scrumptious golden brown sweet waffles crisp on the outside and light inside served with sweet, salty, sticky, buttery sauce.

Preparation time: 4 hours (including resting time) Cooking time: 15-20 minutes per waffle Makes: 4

ingredients

For the waffles:

13 tbsp / 200 gm refined flour
1 tsp / 5 gm salt
½ tbsp / 8 gm baking powder
1 egg, separated
4 tbsp / 60 gm caster sugar
1 cup / 250 ml milk
3¼ tbsp / 50 ml cream
5 tsp / 20 gm yogurt
1 tsp / 5 ml vanilla essence
2½ tbsp / 40 ml melted butter

For the salted caramel sauce:

6 tbsp / 90 ml cream
¼ tsp vanilla beans
7 tbsp / 110 gm caster sugar
2¼ tbsp / 35 ml water
1 tbsp / 15 gm butter
¼ tsp sea salt

method

1. **For the waffles**, sift the flour, salt and baking powder into a bowl. Set aside. In another bowl, whisk the egg yolk with the caster sugar till smooth. Mix the milk, cream, yogurt and vanilla essence in a big bowl. Add the egg yolk and sugar mix. Combine well. Add the flour mixture and mix well with a spatula, but do not overdo the mixing. Now mix in the melted butter. Rest the batter for 4-6 hours or overnight in a refrigerator. To make the waffles extra crispy, beat the egg white till medium peaks form and fold into the batter gently just before you pour the batter into the waffle maker.
2. **For the salted caramel**, heat the cream and vanilla beans in the microwave for 2 minutes. Heat the sugar and water in a saucepan over medium heat until the sugar melts and caramelizes. Add the butter and keep whisking till combined. Lastly, add the cream and whisk till thick. Add the salt and mix again.
3. Serve the sauce with hot waffles.

Chef's Tip: *If you add the whipped egg whites the previous night, the waffles won't be as crispy but still great to eat!*

Dark Chocolate Fondant with Raspberry Jam

Chocolate pudding with a gooey-centre topped with a generous amount of raspberry jam... perfect last-minute dessert to rustle up for the unexpected dinner guests.

Preparation time: 15 minutes Cooking time: 4-5 minutes Makes: 4 medium sized ramekins

ingredients

13 tbsp / 200 gm dark chocolate
13 tbsp / 200 gm butter
10 tbsp / 150 gm caster sugar
4 eggs
4 tbsp / 60 gm refined flour
4 tsp / 20 gm raspberry jam

method

1. Melt the chocolate and butter over a hot water bath or in the microwave.
2. Add the caster sugar and mix well. Allow to cool.
3. Then add the eggs, one by one, whisking well after each addition.
4. Fold in the flour and pour the batter into 4 greased ramekins. Bake in a 200°C / 390°F preheated oven for 4-5 minutes.
5. Take the ramekins out and put 1 tsp of raspberry jam in the centre of each. Return the ramekins back to the oven and bake for another 4-5 minutes or until the edges are cooked but the centre remains wobbly.
6. Remove and serve hot.

Chef's Tip: *Make sure the best quality dark chocolate is used as it is the star ingredient and will make all the difference.*

Falooda-inspired Rose Chia Pudding

Chilled chia pudding flavoured with rose syrup and topped with nuts and pomegranate. A healthy summer cooler.

Preparation time: Overnight   Cooking time: N/A   Makes: 1 glass

ingredients

1 cup / 250 ml milk
4 tsp / 20 gm chia seeds (*sabja* seeds)
1 tsp / 5 ml vanilla essence
A pinch salt
1-2 tsp / 5-10 ml rose syrup
Nuts, as per choice, for topping
A handful pomegranate seeds, for topping

method

1. Mix the milk and chia seeds together in a bowl and refrigerate overnight.
2. Stir in the vanilla essence and salt the next day.
3. Transfer the contents into a bowl or glass and serve with a dash of rose syrup topped with nuts and pomegranate seeds.

GRESHAM FERNANDES is the executive chef, Fine Dine of Impresario Hospitality, the company owning restaurants such as Salt Water Café in Mumbai, Smoke House Room and Smoke House Deli in Delhi and Stone Water Grill in Pune. After a short stint at Copenhagen's celebrated restaurant Noma, Fernandes is now back in Mumbai and continues to helm the kitchens at Salt Water Café.

KELVIN CHEUNG is a Chinese-Canadian chef who was associated with Mumbai's top restaurant Ellipsis before moving back to Toronto and Chicago. After launching One Street Over soon after coming back to India, Chef Kelvin is now a consultant at the seafood restaurant Bastian, in Mumbai.

ZORAWAR KALRA is one of the youngest restaurateurs of India. He has recently been recognized amongst the 50 Most Influential Young Indians by GQ India. He was awarded the title of 'Restaurateur of the Year Award, 2014', at HT Crystals, in 2014 and 'Entrepreneur of the Year in Service Business – F&B Services', at Entrepreneur India Awards in 2014.

SABYASACHI GORAI, popularly known as Chef Saby, owns and runs a boutique consultancy company called Fabrica by Chef Saby in New Delhi. In his two-decade career, beginning at Hotel Guest line, Mumbai, he became the executive chef of one of South East Asia's largest entertainment centres, The Bowling Company, Mumbai, in 1999. Chef Saby received the 'Best Chef of India' award by the then President of India, Pratibha Patil, during the National Tourism Awards 2011–12.

POOJA DHINGRA is an Indian pastry chef and businesswoman. She is the founder of macaron bakery chain Le15 Patisserie and Studio Fifteen Culinary Centre in Mumbai. Pooja was on *Forbes India's* prestigious '30 under 30 list' in 2014, and has been voted a Rising Star by GC Watches and featured in its global campaign. She published her first cookbook, *The Big Book of Treats*, in 2014.

Index

modern european

asian

contemporary indian

mediterranean

desserts

recipes courtesy
Gresham Fernandes, Kelvin Cheung, Zorawar Kalra,
Sabyasachi Gorai, Pooja Dhingra

design
Misha Oberoi

photography
Anshika Varma
Amrita Diwanji for Kelvin Cheung's profile image (pg. 50)

editors
Neeta Datta, Neelam Narula

project coordinator
Anisha Saigal

pre-press
Joyti Dey

production
Yuvraj Singh

for the love of food for the love of food for the love of food for the love of food for the love of food for th

ove of food for the love of food for the love of food for the love of food for the love of food for the love of
for the love of food for the love of food for the love of food for the love of food for the love of food for th
ove of food for the love of food for the love of food for the love of food for the love of food for the love of
for the love of food for the love of food for the love of food for the love of food for the love of food for th
ove of food for the love of food for the love of food for the love of food for the love of food for the love of
for the love of food for the love of food for the love of food for the love of food for the love of food for th
ove of food for the love of food for the love of food for the love of food for the love of food for the love of
for the love of food for the love of food for the love of food for the love of food for the love of food for th
ove of food for the love of food for the love of food for the love of food for the love of food for the love of
for the love of food for the love of food for the love of food for the love of food for the love of food for th
ove of food for the love of food for the love of food for the love of food for the love of food for the love of
for the love of food for the love of food for the love of food for the love of food for the love of food for th
ove of food for the love of food for the love of food for the love of food for the love of food for the love of
for the love of food for the love of food for the love of food for the love of food for the love of food for th
ove of food for the love of food for the love of food for the love of food for the love of food for the love of
for the love of food for the love of food for the love of food for the love of food for the love of food for th
ove of food for the love of food for the love of food for the love of food for the love of food for the love of
for the love of food for the love of food for the love of food for the love of food for the love of food for th
ove of food for the love of food for the love of food for the love of food for the love of food for the love of
for the love of food for the love of food for the love of food for the love of food for the love of food for th
ove of food for the love of food for the love of food for the love of food for the love of food for the love of
for the love of food for the love of food for the love of food for the love of food for the love of food for th
ove of food for the love of food for the love of food for the love of food for the love of food for the love of
for the love of food for the love of food for the love of food for the love of food for the love of food for th
ove of food for the love of food for the love of food for the love of food for the love of food for the love of
for the love of food for the love of food for the love of food for the love of food for the love of food for th
ove of food for the love of food for the love of food for the love of food for the love of food for the love of